NORTH CAROLINA MOONSHINE

AN ILLICIT HISTORY

Frank Stephenson Jr. & Barbara Nichols Mulder

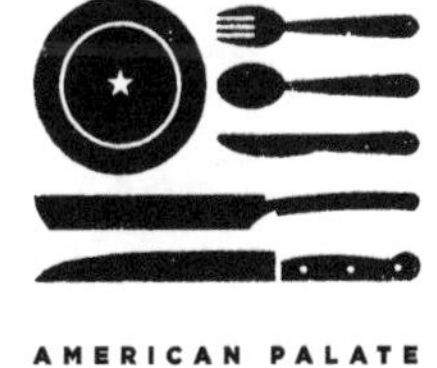

Published by American Palate
A Division of The History Press
Charleston, SC
www.historypress.net

First published 2017

ISBN 9781540214102

Library of Congress Control Number: 2016950689

Notice: The information in this book is true and complete to the best of our knowledge. It is offered without guarantee on the part of the authors or The History Press. The authors and The History Press disclaim all liability in connection with the use of this book.

This book is dedicated to the two groups of individuals who were responsible for North Carolina having one of the most colorful and greatest moonshine legacies of any state in the history of the United States. The two groups are the moonshiners who made the moonshine and the local, state and federal moonshine raiders who, for years and years, chased them all across North Carolina, from Manteo to Murphy, South Mills to Highlands, Waterlilly to Maxton, Warren Plains to Bakersfield, Weldon to Waxhaw, Maney's Neck to Swannanoa, New Holland to West Jefferson, Enfield to Robbinsville and Morehead City to Marble.

CONTENTS

ACKNOWLEDGEMENTS

The authors acknowledge with grateful appreciation the generous help and assistance from the following:

Adrian Denny, Rapid City, South Dakota
Al Bullard, Evansville, Indiana
Albert Cummings, Edenton, North Carolina
Alfred Deanes, Waynesboro, Virginia
Allen Compton, Wise, Virginia
Allen Draper, Silver Springs, Maryland
Anthony Buck, Sarasota, Florida
Anthony Spearman, Durham, North Carolina
Arnold Fogler, Waterlilly, North Carolina
Arron Rowman, Springfield, Virginia
Ashley Sediak-Propst, Historic Cabarrus Association, Concord, North Carolina
Aurelius Johnson, Laredo, Texas
Axel Winder, Dover, Delaware
Balcolm Crawford, Paris, France
Barbara Jean Mulder, Conway, North Carolina
Beryl Rothman, Rapid City, South Dakota
Biggs Funeral Home, Lumberton, North Carolina
Blair Hammett, Raleigh, North Carolina
Brad Call, Call Family Distillery, Wilkesboro, North Carolina
Brandon Duke, Franklin, Virginia

Acknowledgements

Brock Janney, Kinston, North Carolina
Bryant Coker, Lexington, Virginia
Buck Noble, Anderson, South Carolina
Buford Pope, St. Paul, Minnesota
Burton Rogerson, Tulsa, Oklahoma
Caroline Stephenson, Como, North Carolina
Charles Ridley, Barstow, California
Chester Allport, Albany, New York
Christinia Perry, Popcorn Sutton Distilling, Cleveland, Ohio
Chuck Pergonnie, Oxford, North Carolina
Clayton Burns, Hickory, North Carolina
Curtis and Rose Nichols, Suffolk, Virginia
Dallas Griffin, Mobile, Alabama
Dalton Anthony, Emporia, Virginia
Daniel Bowling, London, England
David Cain, Manchester, New Hampshire
David Radcliff, Dover, Delaware
David Twiford, Twiford Funeral Home, Elizabeth City, North Carolina
Delbert Eagleton, Reno, Nevada
Dismal Swamp State Park, South Mills, North Carolina
Dock Clements, Boise, Idaho
Donald Douglas, Robesonian, Lumberton, North Carolina
Dr. Pamela Price Mitchern, Belk Library, Appalachian State University, Boone, North Carolina
Dr. Robert Anthony, North Carolina Collection, UNC–Chapel Hill, Chapel Hill, North Carolina
Earl Raeford, Norfolk, Virginia
Eddie Lee Hampton, Asheville, North Carolina
Eddie Paulsen, New Bern, North Carolina
Eddie Weaver, South Boston, Virginia
Edmond W. Caldwell Jr., North Carolina Sheriffs' Association, Raleigh, North Carolina
Ed Robinette, Kannapolis History Museum, Kannapolis, North Carolina
Edward Garrison, Raleigh, North Carolina
Elise Allison, Greensboro Historical Museum, Greensboro, North Carolina
Elmore Duggins, Whiteville, North Carolina
Elridge Furgerson, Kinston, North Carolina
Elton Bracey, Danville, Virginia
Emmett Wiggins, Lake Placid, New York

Acknowledgements

Emmit Bourgrande, High Point, North Carolina
Ernest Broadway, Spartanburg, South Carolina
Ernie Gregory, Lumberton, North Carolina
Eugene Bowman, Bozeman, Montana
The family of Charles Sylvester Felts, Boone, North Carolina
Franklin Brabben, Miami, Florida
Fulton Thomas, Long Island, New York
Gerald Anderson, Clinton, North Carolina
Gerry DeArmond, New Hanover Public Library, Wilmington, North Carolina
Grayson Ray, Buffalo, New York
Greta Browning, Belk Library, Appalachian State University, Boone, North Carolina
Grover Jenkins, Far Rockaway, New York
Guy Johnson, Bakersville, California
Hampton Lewis, Wilmington, Delaware
Harold Jacobs, Dallas, Texas
Harrison Boone, Melbourne, Florida
Irwin Lindsay, Denver, Colorado
Jake Odom, Conway, North Carolina
Jason Baucombe, Durham, North Carolina
Jerry Cahoon, Manteo, North Carolina
Jerry Weaver, Charlottesville, Virginia
Jochen Kunstler, Como, North Carolina
John Hobarth, Hamlet, North Carolina
John L. Stephenson, Murfreesboro, North Carolina
Johnny Binkley, Raleigh, North Carolina,
Jordan Chapman, St. Louis, Missouri
Joseph Hullen, Reidsville, North Carolina
Juewn Tomberlin, North Carolina Collection, UNC–Chapel Hill, Chapel Hill, North Carolina
Justin Rumbach, *Jasper (IN) Herald*
Justin Shelton, Belk Library, Appalachian State University, Boone, North Carolina
Kathleen Monahan, Wilson Library, UNC–Chapel Hill, Chapel Hill, North Carolina
Keith Longiotti, North Carolina Collection, UNC–Chapel Hill, Chapel Hill, North Carolina
Kim Anderson, North Carolina Department of Cultural Resources, Raleigh, North Carolina
Lance Jefferson, Denver, Colorado

Acknowledgements

Layton Chambers, Kings Mountain, North Carolina
Lee Rammick, Providence, Rhode Island
Leland Braxton, Shelby, North Carolina
Lemuel Spain, Rocky Mount, Virginia
Len Tuttle, Gastonia, North Carolina
Leonard Browning, Hickory, North Carolina
Leon Daughtrey, Elkins, West Virginia
Lesley Wayne, Washington, North Carolina
Leta Phelps, Popcorn Sutton Distilling, Newport, Tennessee
Licensed Beverage Industries, New York, New York
Linda Hassell, Whitaker Library, Chowan University, Murfreesboro, North Carolina
Lindsey Carr, Society Hill, South Carolina
Lisa Wall, *Morganton News Herald*, Morganton, North Carolina
Livingston Sumner, Como, North Carolina
Lloyd Breland, Lawrenceville, Virginia
Lucus Ellison, Elkins, North Carolina
Luke Monzell, Fargo, North Dakota
Madison Furlough, Spokane, Washington
Malcohn Jeffers, Norfolk, Virginia
Malcolm McLeod Jr., Greenville, North Carolina
Manuel Kiser, Kannapolis, North Carolina
Marcus Johnston, Albemarle, North Carolina
Marcus Owens, Cape May, New Jersey
Martha Elmore, Special Collections, Joyner Library, East Carolina University
Marty Wise, Rocky Mount, Virginia
Matthew Turi, Southern Historical Collection, UNC–Chapel Hill, Chapel Hill, North Carolina
Matthew Wachna, North Carolina Department of Cultural Resources, Raleigh, North Carolina
Matthew Wilder, Providence, Rhode Island
Matt Provancha, Mountain Gateway Museum, Old Fort, North Carolina
Maury Lane, Montgomery, Alabama
Mel Bosco, Jefferson City, Tennessee
Merchants Mill State Park, Gatesville, North Carolina
Monroe Hatcher, Jackson, Mississippi
Morgan Vickery, Goldsboro, North Carolina
Nance Seymour, Sioux City, Iowa
Napeleon Whitaker, Rockingham, North Carolina

Nash Brannon, Morgantown, West Virginia
Neal Hutcheson, Sucker Punch Pictures, Raleigh, North Carolina
Neil Hutcheson, Sucker Punch Pictures, Raleigh, North Carolina
Nelson Abbott, Bryson City, North Carolina
Nick Ripson, Toronto, Canada
Norman Bellinger, Danville, Virginia
North Carolina Law Enforcement Women's Association, Durham, North Carolina
Patrick Mucklow, Museum of Durham History, Durham, North Carolina
Paul Hightower, Mooresville, North Carolina
Perry Sullivan, Lake St. Louis, Missouri
Peter Dirkson, Rockport, Maine
Peter Gyimesi, Popcorn Sutton Distilling, Columbus, Ohio
Phillip McGuire, Boone, North Carolina
Rainey Danneller, Wilmington, North Carolina
Ralph Davis, Murfreesboro, North Carolina
Ralph Duvall, Wanchese, North Carolina
Randall Holmes, Manteo, North Carolina
Raymond Ellis, Mobile, Alabama
Richard Cagle, Winston-Salem, North Carolina
Richmond County Historical Society, Rockingham, North Carolina
Roger Beckman, Knoxville, Tennessee
Roger Tinsdale, Detroit, Michigan
Roland Byers, Dayton, Ohio
Roland Skippers, Morehead City, North Carolina
Ronald Bryant, Lincolnton, North Carolina
Ronald Duggins, Wadesboro, North Carolina
Ross Jenkins, Atlanta, Georgia
Roy Higgenbotham, Salt Lake City, Utah
Ryan Coltrane, Kansas City, Missouri
Ryland Peterson, Chicago, Illinois
Sarah Pockmire, Moore County Historical Society, Southern Pines, North Carolina.
Shelley McBride, Kannapolis History Museum, Kannapolis, North Carolina
Sheriff's Office, Robeson County, Lumberton, North Carolina
Spencer Edmonds, Norlina, North Carolina
The staff at Dare County Public Library, Manteo, North Carolina
The staff at Milwaukee Public Library, Milwaukee, Wisconsin
The staff at Richmond Public Library, Richmond, Virginia

Acknowledgements

Stephen Barrow, Kittrell, North Carolina
Stephen Fletcher, North Carolina Collection, UNC–Chapel Hill, Chapel Hill, North Carolina
Stuart Parks, Outer Banks History Center, Manteo, North Carolina
Ted Baucombe, Yonkers, New York
Teddy Albertson, Fillmore, California
Terry Maxwell, Mobile, Alabama
Thomas Bosher, Lincoln, Nebraska
Thomas Wentworth, Martinsville, Virginia
Tobin Jackson, New Orleans, Louisiana
Tom Bill Daniels, Margaretville, North Carolina
Victor Hightower, Clinton, North Carolina
Virgil Monroe, Fayetteville, North Carolina
Vito Gabriel, Stillwater, Oklahoma
Vito Nicholson, Palm Beach, Florida
Wanda Lassiter, Museum of the Albemarle, Elizabeth City, North Carolina
Warren Houser, Frankfort, Kentucky
Wayne Burden, Taos, New Mexico
Wesley Davis, Belk Library, Appalachian State University, Boone, North Carolina
William Turner, New Brunswick, New Jersey
Will Romine, Old Trap, North Carolina
Wilson Hamilton, Charlotte, North Carolina
Wilson Laney, Fredericksburg, Virginia
Zoe Rhine and staff, North Carolina Collection, Pack Memorial Library, Asheville, North Carolina

Introduction
A State of Moonshine

North Carolina is known for such famous people as Ava Gardner, Richard Petty, Dale Earnhardt and Thomas Wolfe and such cultural exports as tobacco, furniture, NASCAR and, last but not least, moonshine. Why is gritty moonshine included on this iconic North Carolina list? The making of moonshine is one of the state's oldest industries and often has been called the second-oldest profession in North Carolina. Furthermore, over the years, moonshine has captured the imagination, fascination and curiosity of North Carolinians in such a way that some people have gotten hooked on it without drinking a drop of it. Some Tar Heels became so enthralled with the mystic drink that they became moonshine junkies. People all across North Carolina, from socialites to the good ole boys, were and remain enamored of the illegal manufacture of whiskey and the many sidebars that came to be associated with what we all call moonshine. The very mention of moonshine in North Carolina often brings to mind anecdotes of all descriptions. Although the widespread manufacture of moonshine across North Carolina is over, the topic remains as popular as ever with writers, publishers and the media.

There is not another state in the United States that has a richer, broader, deeper or more colorful moonshine history and heritage than North Carolina. From the bourbon-colored waters of the Chowan River in eastern North Carolina to the rocky Neuse River in the piedmont and the cold, clear waters of the French Broad River in the mountains, moonshine has been a way of life and culture for more than three centuries. The lowland and swampy nature of the state's coastal plains section, along with the rolling

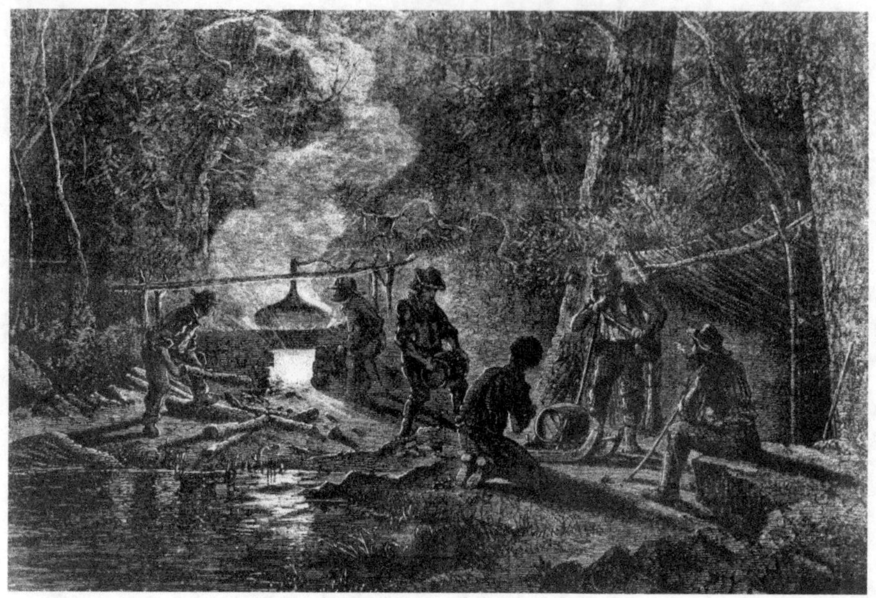

Drawing of the *Southern Mode of Making Whisky* from *Harper's Weekly*, December 7, 1867. *Courtesy of the State Archives of North Carolina.*

back country of the piedmont and the hills and hollers of the mountainous section of western North Carolina, provided Tar Heel bootleggers with near perfect locales for making stump juice.

Moonshine has been made in the Tar Heel state ever since European settlers arrived here, bringing with them their old-country techniques and recipes for making alcohol. In the colonial era and well into the nineteenth century, the whiskey still was an accepted fixture on most homesteads in the state. Indeed, an examination of the state's old records reveals that one of the most prized possessions on the small farm or large plantation, regardless of the landowner, was the still. In swamps, forests, caves, hollers, barns, houses and just anywhere imaginable, North Carolina moonshiners turned corn into whiskey. North Carolina moonshiners made top-quality liquor and were proud of it, even though they broke tax laws and ran a high risk of arrest, going to jail and losing a source of income.

Until the Civil War, no law forbade and no tax hindered the making of whiskey in North Carolina. The colonial-period settlers of North Carolina were adept at making whiskey. Their product was used in daily life. Laborers were sometimes paid with whiskey, and in the early years of the colony, traders exchanged whiskey with the Native Americans on the frontier. Locally made corn liquor was also a given part of most social events. Corn whiskey was

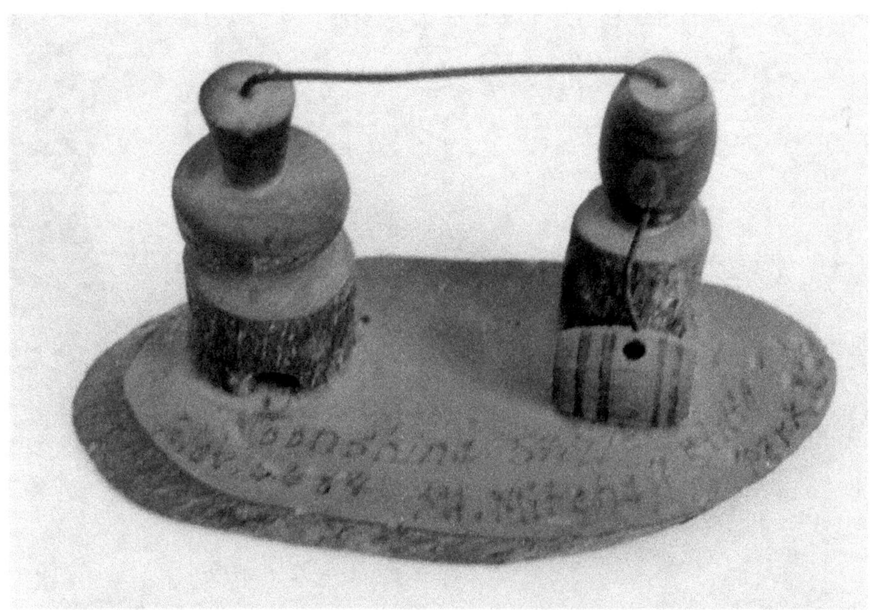

This souvenir model still from Mount Mitchell, North Carolina, was given to Frank Stephenson by his mother, Lucye B. Stephenson. The model still was given to her by her mother-in-law, Tiny G. Stephenson. *Photograph by Frank Stephenson Jr.*

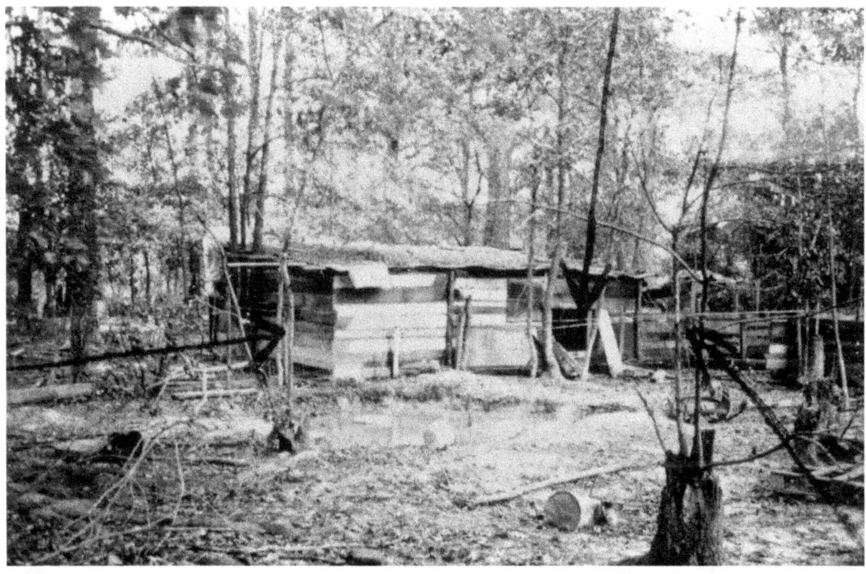

Liquor stills in North Carolina were found everywhere; this one was found beneath a hog pen near Windsor in 1970 by Hertford County ABC officer Calvin Pearce and Bertie County ABC officer Jesse Johnson. *Courtesy of Calvin Pearce.*

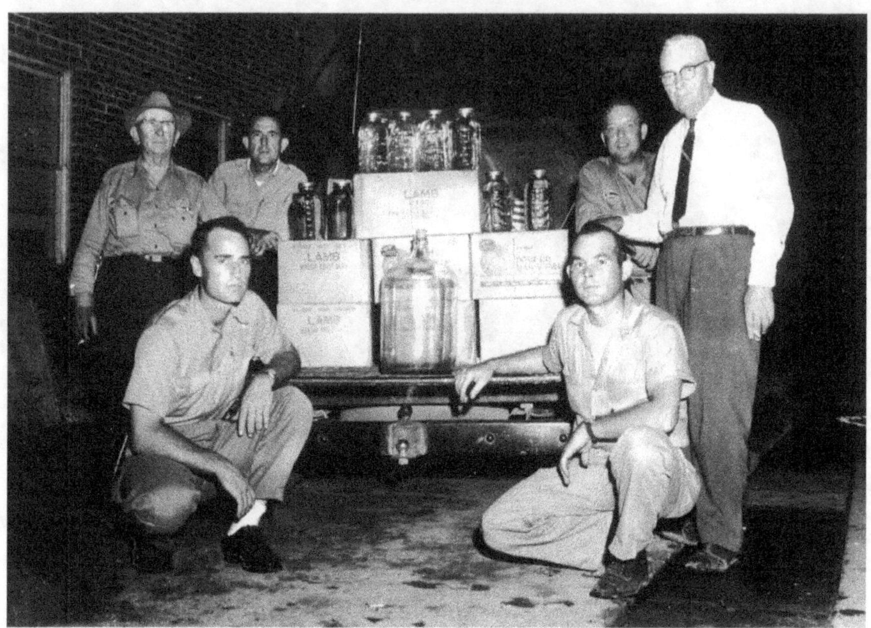

A familiar scene that was repeated many times across North Carolina: moonshine raiders proudly pose with the bounty of their raids. Hertford County moonshine raiders are shown in Winton in July 1959 with bootleg they seized near Harrellsville. *Courtesy of Frank Stephenson Jr.*

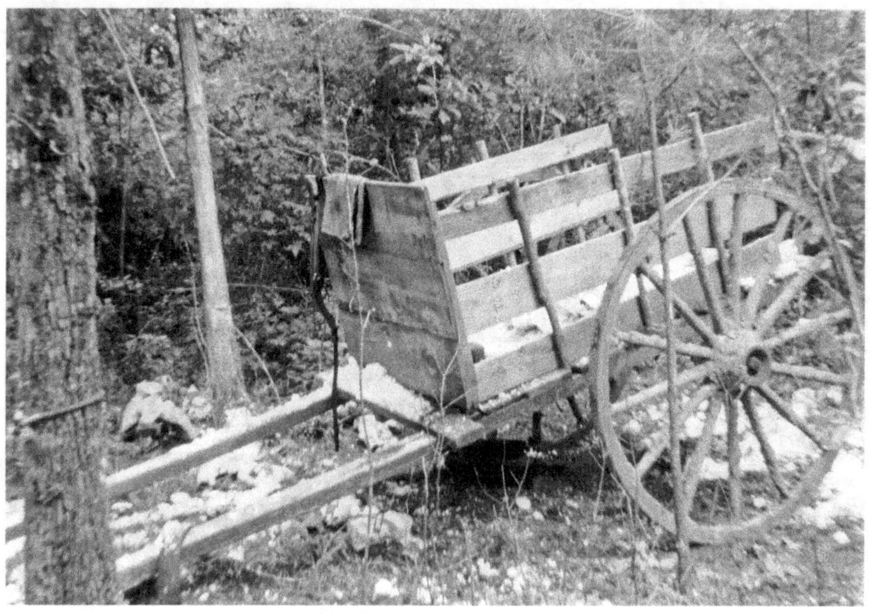

This cart was found at a still that ATF raided in Bertie County in July 1965. *Courtesy of James Saunders.*

Right: Some North Carolina fruitcake makers, including the one that made this fruitcake, preferred to power up their products by adding moonshine to the mix. *Photograph by Frank Stephenson Jr.*

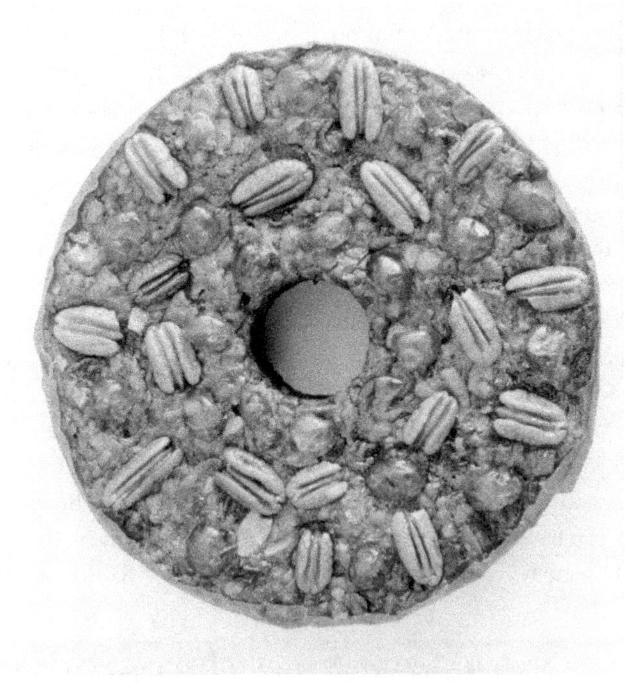

Below: It does not pay to keep an operating still in your house; it could catch the house on fire and burn it down, which is exactly what happened in 1956 to a bootlegger who was located four miles south of Murfreesboro. *Courtesy of Frank Stephenson Jr.*

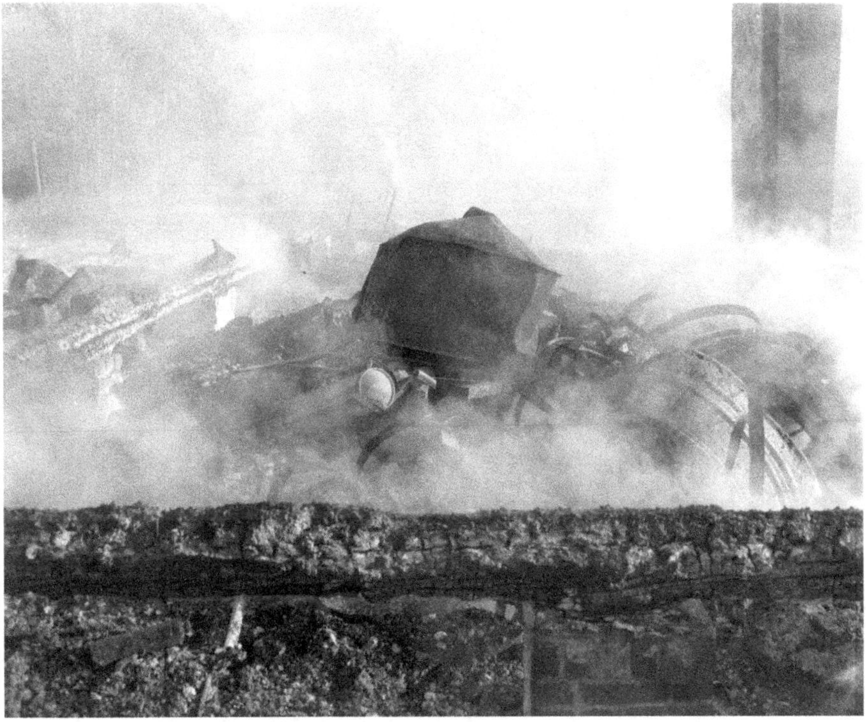

also used for medicinal purposes. Ralph Davis, a miller at Worrell's gristmill in Murfreesboro, told Frank Stephenson Jr. that "the best cure for a cold was a tablespoon of honey and a tablespoon of lemon juice all stirred up in a small glass of Carolina moonshine." Davis explained, "Two good snorts of moonshine sure did wonders for my lumbago."

The unencumbered manufacturing of corn whiskey came to an end on July 1, 1862, when Congress passed the act that is the basis for our present tax system and created the Office of Internal Revenue. This led to the imposing of taxes on distilled spirits, the first being in 1863 for $0.20 a gallon to pay for the cost of the Civil War. The act also provided for the first federal revenue agents. Individuals could not make whiskey without paying a tax. North Carolina distillers became the subject of the federal tax when the state rejoined the Union following the end of the Civil War. Congress raised the tax to $1.50 per gallon in 1865. The tax was raised again in 1866 to $2.00 per gallon and to 1,000 percent of the original costs in 1868. The heavy taxation on distilled spirits led to the creation of an enormous

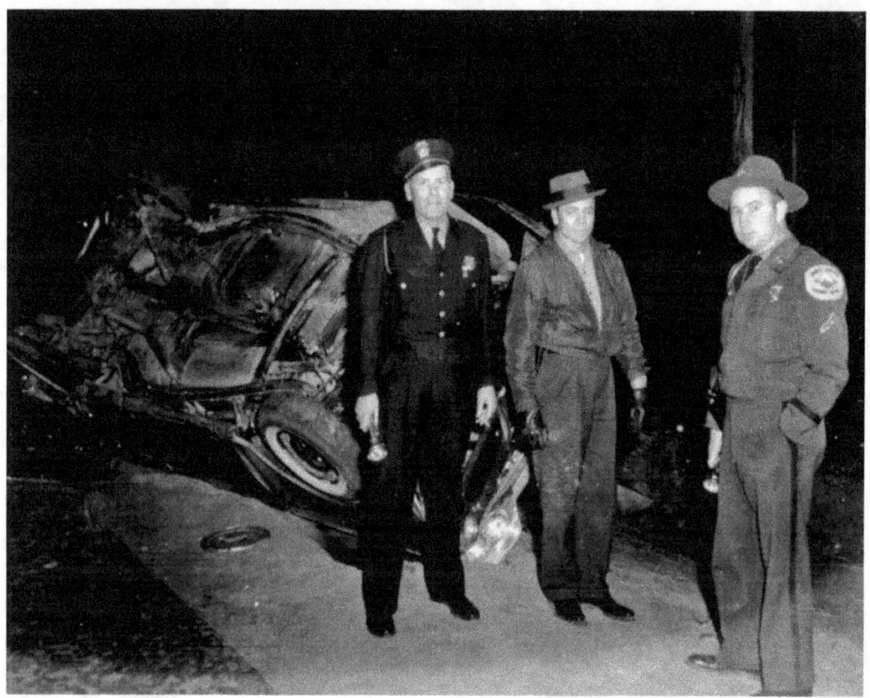

This moonshine runner, who was being pursued in April 1956 by two North Carolina state troopers, did not make it across the Virginia state line. *Courtesy of Frank Stephenson Jr.*

clandestine moonshine industry that would not slow down until over one hundred years later.

Today, there are probably a few small stills operating in far, isolated corners of North Carolina. But there was a time when rivers of moonshine flowed all across the state and making bootleg whiskey became a way of life and culture of its own. The early 1900s through the 1970s were huge years for the production of moonshine across North Carolina. The state was part of what was called the Moonshine Belt, where most of the moonshine in the United States was produced. The Moonshine Belt comprised the states of the old South: Alabama, Georgia, Mississippi, North Carolina, South Carolina, Tennessee and Virginia.

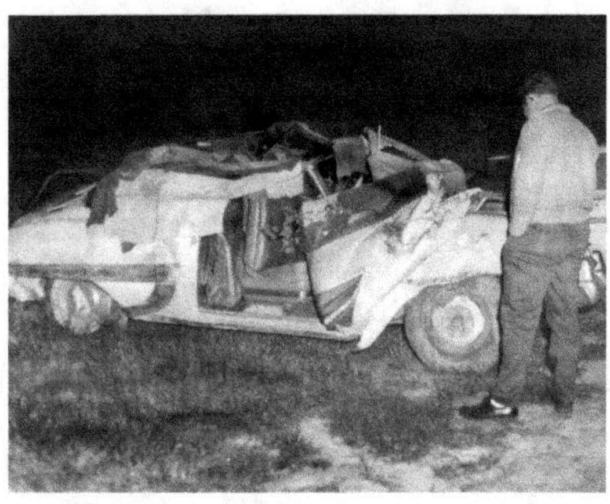

Another load of moonshine did not make it to Virginia while being chased by Northampton County ABC officers in March 1958 on U.S. 301 north of Garysburg. *Courtesy of Frank Stephenson Jr.*

Franklin County, Virginia, and Wilkes County, North Carolina, were always squabbling over which was the Moonshine Capital of the United States. It is generally recognized by most moonshine observers that Wilkes County, North Carolina, deserved the title. When things got too hot for some of the larger bootleggers in Wilkes County, they and some other high-powered moonshiners around the state sought out other locations to put down their stills. One of these locations was eastern North Carolina, where some of the largest rigs ever found were linked to mountain or central North Carolina bootleggers. Moonshine was made in each of North Carolina's one hundred counties, and some, including Wilkes, Madison, Johnston and Harnett, became known as havens for bootleggers.

The three key elements for a location to be good for making moonshine—plentiful water supply, isolation and a thick overhead canopy—were all found in abundance across North Carolina. Many bootleggers preferred to place their stills under holly trees because the thick growth of holly leaves thinned the rising smoke, making it less noticeable. The thick growth of rhododendron in the mountain section of North Carolina provided a near perfect hiding place for stills. The isolation and rugged

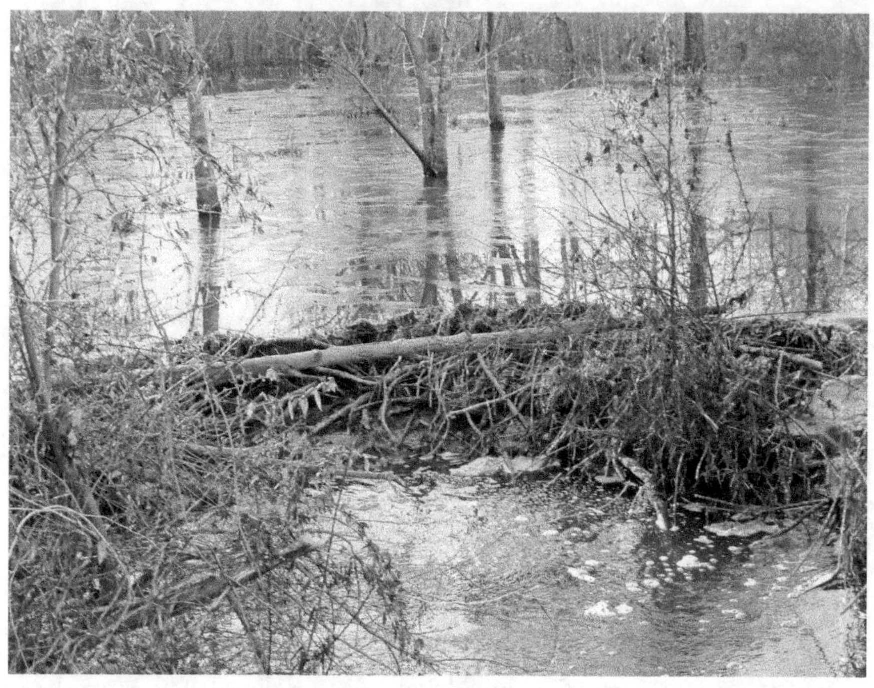

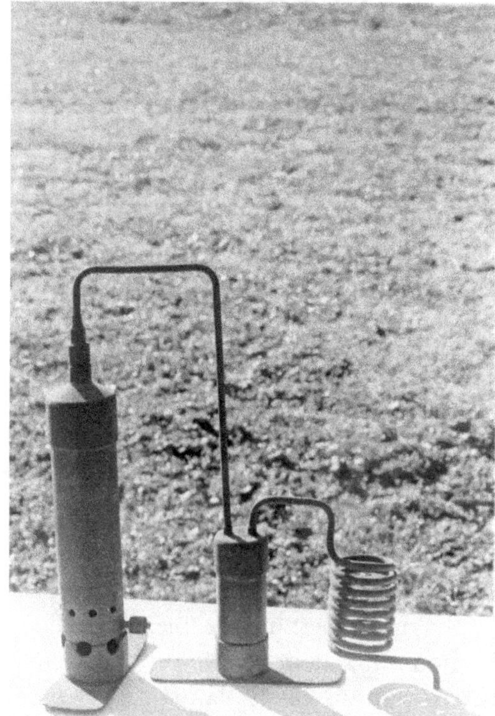

Above: North Carolina moonshiners utilized numerous sources to supply water to their stills, including beaver ponds like the one shown here. *Photograph by John L. Stephenson.*

Left: Whiskey stills found in North Carolina came in all sizes, including this Lilliputian-size working still that was seized in Gaston in 1960 by Northampton County deputy Ed Ingram. *Photograph by Frank Stephenson Jr.*

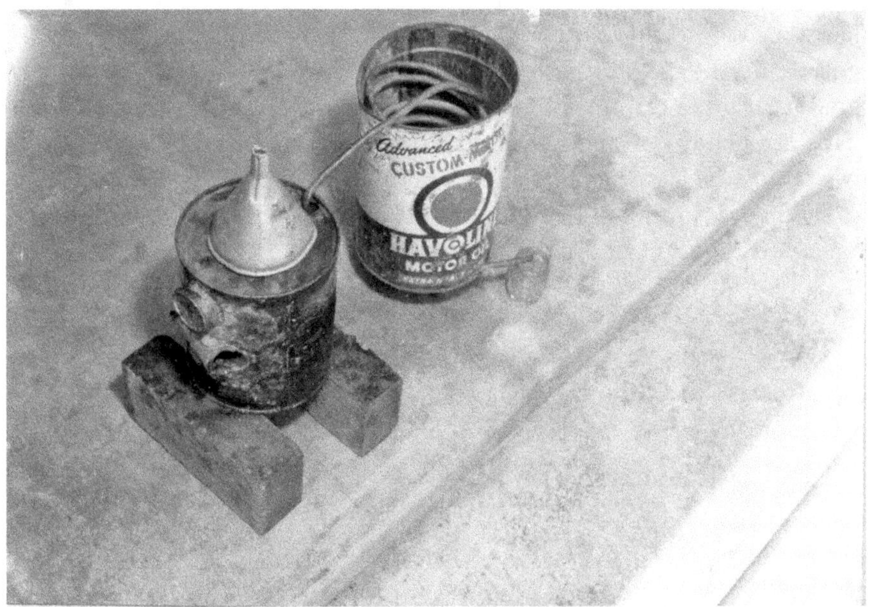

This motor oil can still was captured on a July 30, 1957 raid in Harrellsville by Hertford County deputies Leon Perry and Fred Liverman. *Courtesy of Frank Stephenson Jr.*

backcountry of North Carolina made for a perfect place for moonshiners from within the state and from other locations to put down their stills, thus making the state a mecca for moonshine operations of all sizes.

It is clear from a study of the moonshine operations in North Carolina through the years that the "Noble Experiment," or nationwide Prohibition (1920–33), brought on by the passage of the Volstead Act of 1919 had no major effect on bootlegging in the state. In fact, some of the largest stills ever broken up in the state were found during the Prohibition era. It is also clear that the passage of the Mandatory Preventive Raw Materials Program, which went into effect in 1956, supposedly to put a squeeze on the lifeblood of bootlegging—the sugar supply—and the Container Law of 1959 did not cripple moonshine production in the state. North Carolina had some of the toughest and fiercest moonshine raiders in the nation, and even their valiant and tireless war against moonshiners could not put an end to the huge illegal liquor business because bootleggers found ways around most roadblocks. The two roadblocks that finally spelled the beginning of the end of moonshining as a way of life and culture in North Carolina were the opening of state liquor stores and the rise in use and popularity of illegal drugs, such as marijuana. It is known that some of the later and larger bootleggers left moonshine behind and moved into the illegal drug business in a big way. Many bootleggers just hung it all up and retired from the business since the state liquor stores made it much easier and safer to purchase whiskey.

A few of the former moonshiners, such as Marvin "Pop Corn" Sutton, Alvin Sawyer and Junior Johnson, turned their years of moonshine experience into legal money. Marvin "Pop Corn" Sutton, the Paul

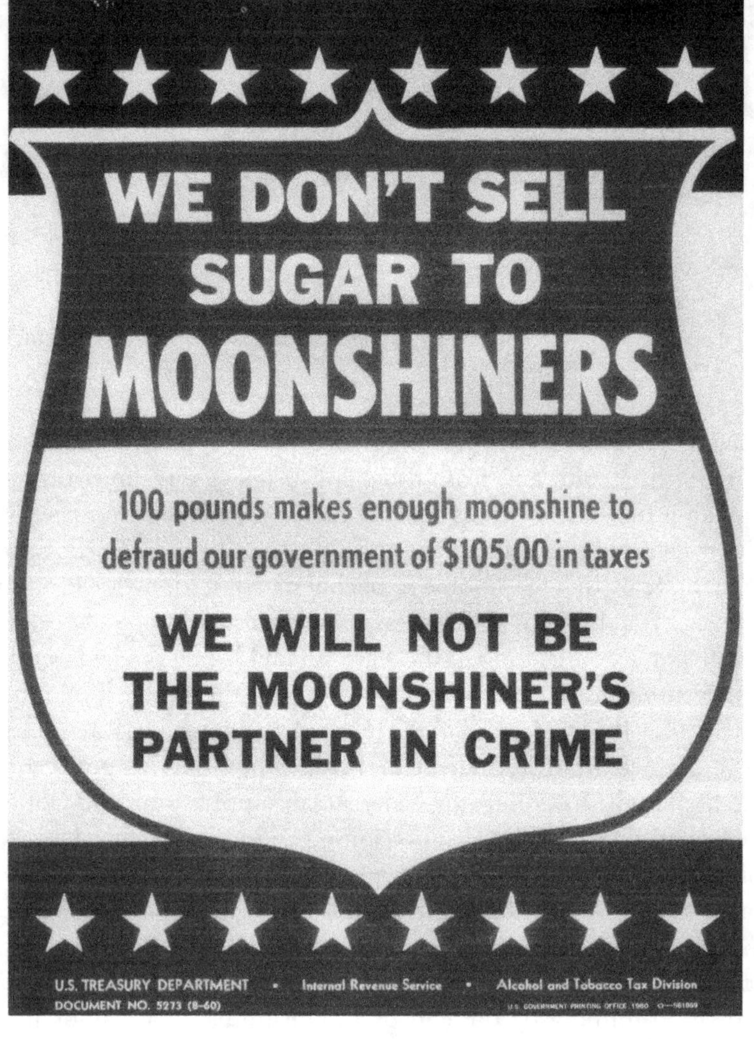

ATF waged a significant war against bootleggers during the moonshine era, and among the many weapons it employed was this grocery store poster. *Courtesy of Phillip McGuire.*

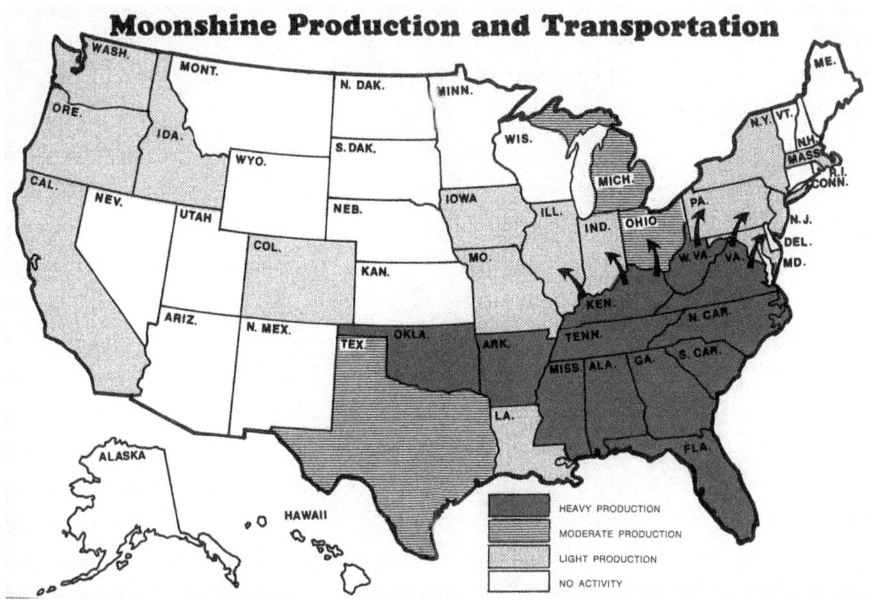

A 1966 moonshine production chart. *Courtesy of Licensed Beverages Industries, New York.*

Bunyan of North Carolina moonshine, became a huge celebrity in the western North Carolina area of Maggie Valley and eastern Tennessee following his retirement from making moonshine. Alvin Sawyer, the Moonshine King of the Great Dismal Swamp, made and sold miniature stills after he retired from making stump juice. Junior Johnson utilized the driving skills he learned while traveling many miles as a moonshine hauler to become one of NASCAR's most popular drivers and a member of its hall of fame. Following his record-setting career with NASCAR, Johnson used his extensive knowledge of moonshine to help develop a legal whiskey distillery, Piedmont Distillers in Madison, North Carolina, that produces his own brand, Midnight Moon Moonshine.

This book provides a gritty glance back at the intriguing profession of the illegal manufacture of whiskey in the Tar Heel state. This book is not about every person who was involved in moonshine or every still that was raided in North Carolina. Furthermore, in this book, we look at the underbelly of making moonshine in North Carolina. A large number of North Carolina stills were never detected while other stills had a little longer than usual operational lifetime because they were protected operations, though these occurrences were rare; 99.9 percent of North Carolina's moonshine raiders were men and women who rode tall in the saddle and whose honesty and integrity were beyond reproach. From their stories, as well as those from some of the shiners they busted, we've culled this history of moonshine in North Carolina.

Chapter 1

COASTAL PLAINS

Rivers of Moonshine

North Carolina's vast coastal plains region extends from the Atlantic Ocean on the east to the piedmont section in the west and the Virginia state line in the north to the South Carolina state line in the south. While the section is home to scores and scores of small towns, it is also home to several medium-size towns and small cities. When the early settlers of the coastal plains region began to filter down in the late 1600s and early 1700s, primarily from counties in southeast Virginia, they brought whiskey-making recipes from the old country with them. Gradually, the production of whiskey in the region began to grow and flourish to such a degree that the region became a major producer of moonshine. In the September 2, 1951 issue of the *Murfreesboro Daily News*, editor F. Roy Johnson wrote, "The four Coastal plains counties of Hertford, Bertie, Northampton and Gates do more than a million dollars a year in bootleg whiskey business and between 1000 to 1500 unlicensed distilleries keep a steady flow of white lightning going to local and out-of-the area thirsty moonshine guzzler[s]." Johnson based his article on personal interviews with the sheriffs and other moonshine busters in the four-county region.

The densely wooded, swampy landscape and the isolated nature of the coastal plains region of North Carolina made it possible for bootleggers to set up their illegal booze plants, and many came from across the state (and even other states) to do so. Some of the stills that the moonshiners set up in the coastal plains region of North Carolina were highly sophisticated. An excellent example of one is the giant moonshine factory that was discovered

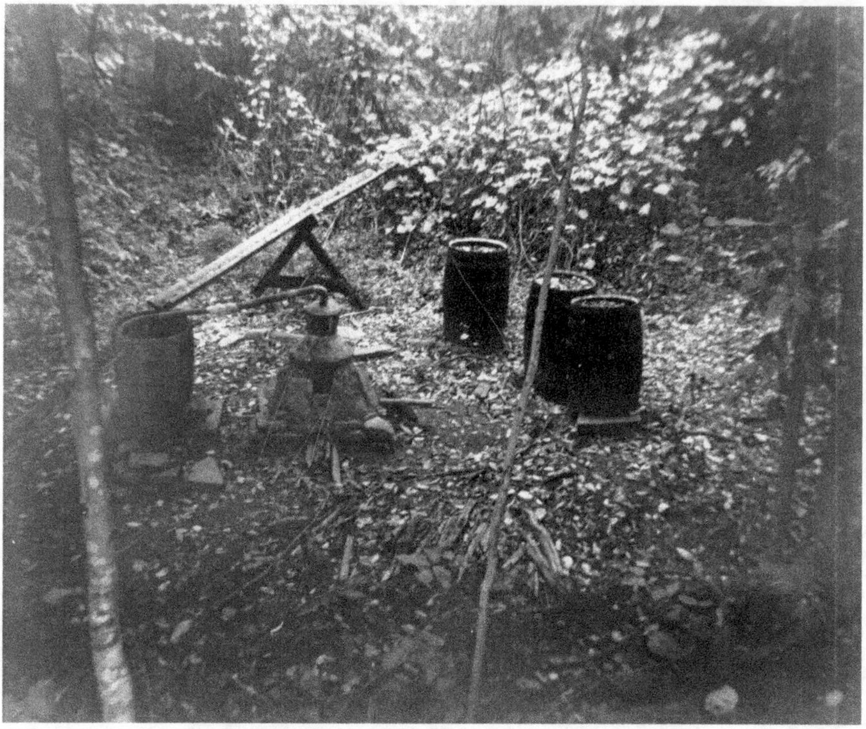

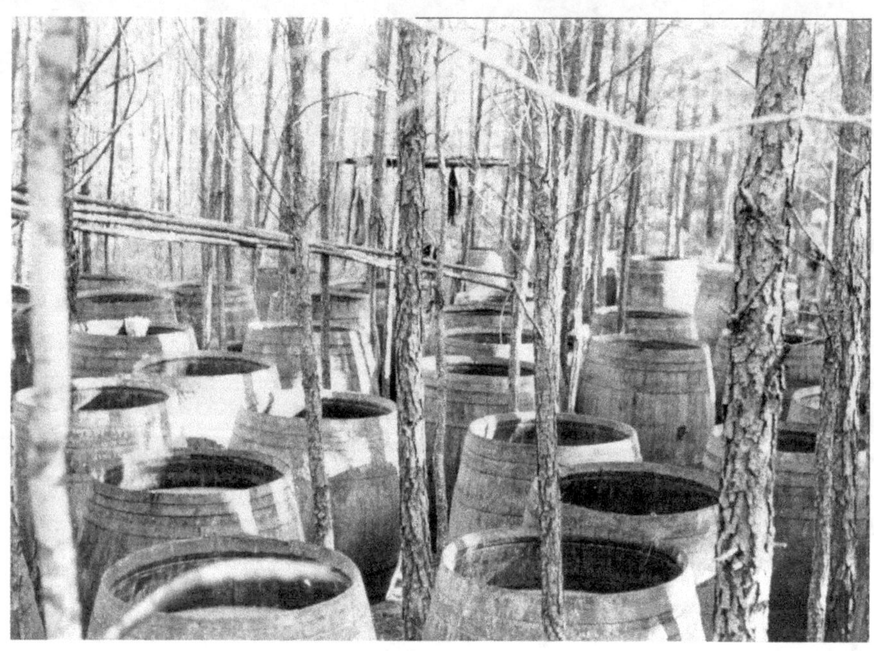

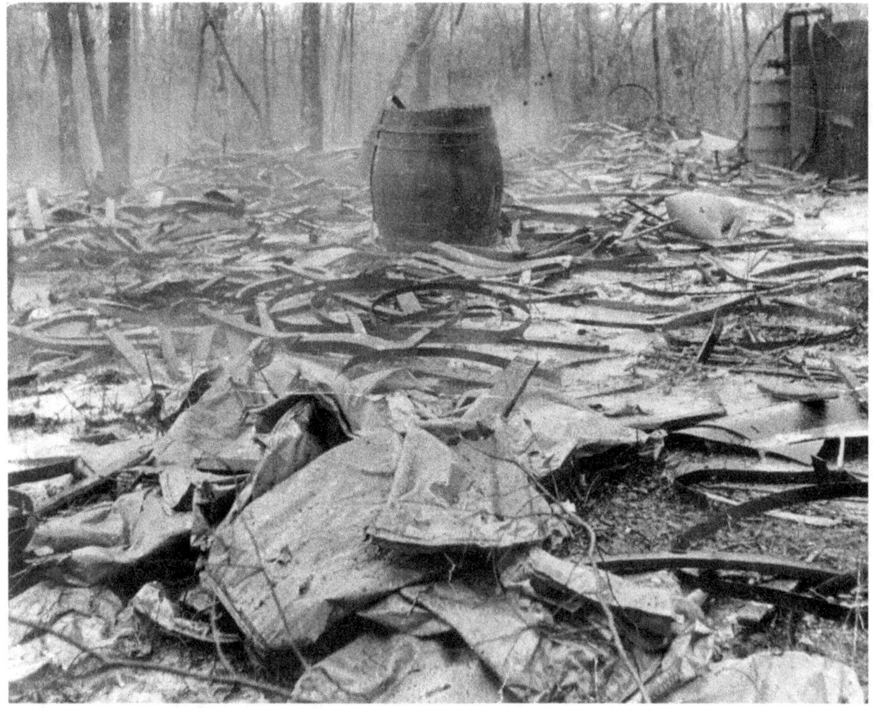

ATF agents used 110 sticks of dynamite to destroy a jumbo still near Murfreeboro in October 1960. Mash and muck were dripping from the trees following the blast, which, for some reason, left one barrel of mash standing. *Courtesy of Fred Liverman.*

Opposite, top: This small still, dating from the 1930s, was found near Tyler's Cave in Northampton County. *Courtesy of Fred Liverman.*

Opposite, bottom: While many North Carolina moonshine stills were small or medium size, much larger stills, such as the one near Murfreesboro where these mash barrels were found in 1960, did exist. *Courtesy of Fred Liverman.*

at Merry Hill in Bertie County in May 1972. The moonshine raiders who discovered this giant still determined its operators were from western North Carolina and eastern Tennessee. A number of the coastal plains stills were capable of producing hundreds of gallons of swamp juice a week; others would run off a jug or two, and the medium-size rigs produced fifty to one hundred gallons weekly. On rare occasions, local moonshine raiders discovered some odd or unusual bootleg operations, such as stovetop stills capable of running off a quart or two a day. These midget rigs were literally set on top of a stove that provided the heat source to cook the mash while the booze operator had all of the comforts of home.

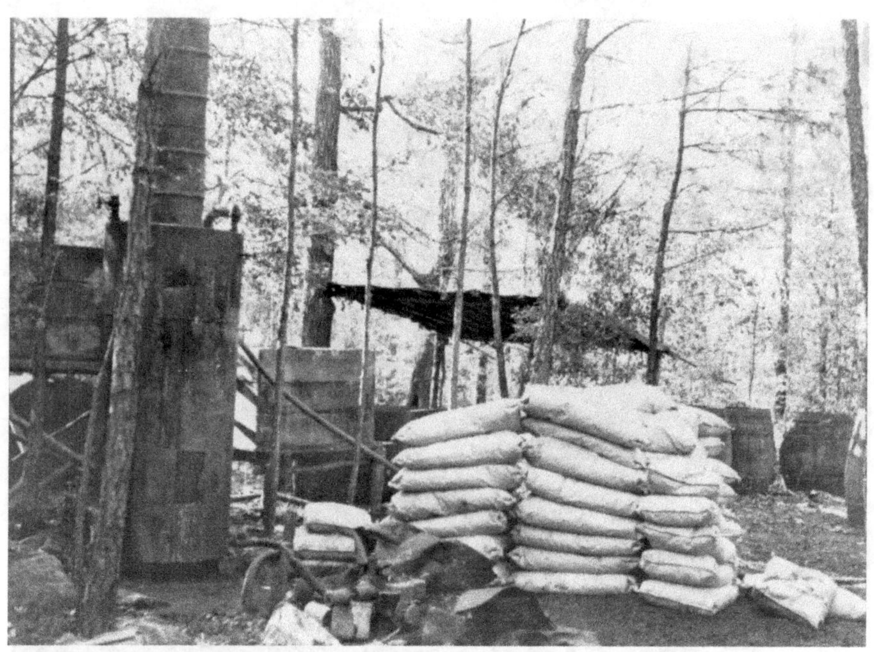

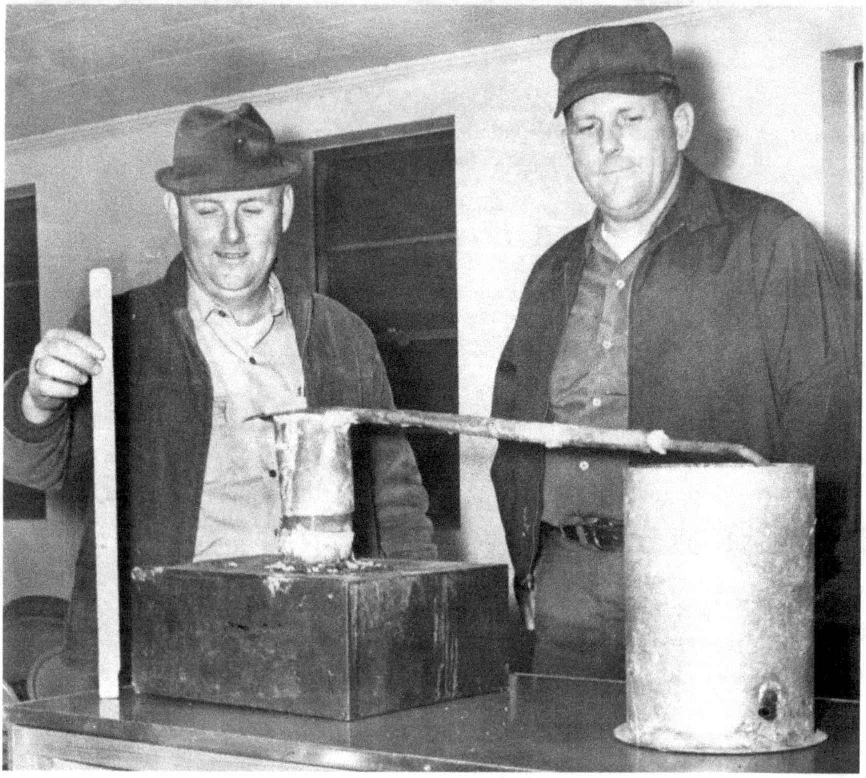

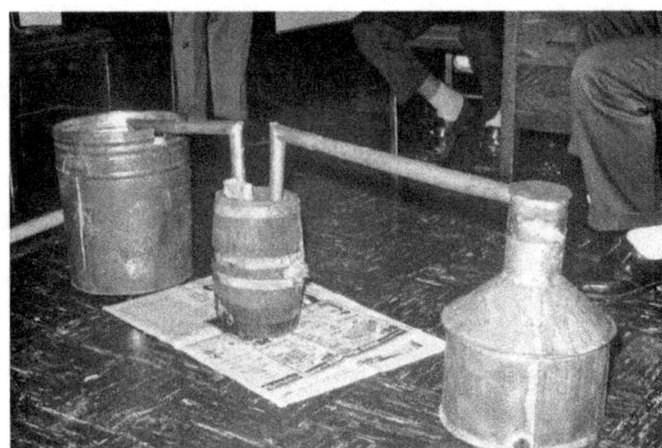

This small still that was captured in Halifax County is another example of the range of still sizes that were utilized by North Carolina moonshiners. *Courtesy of Edward Garrison.*

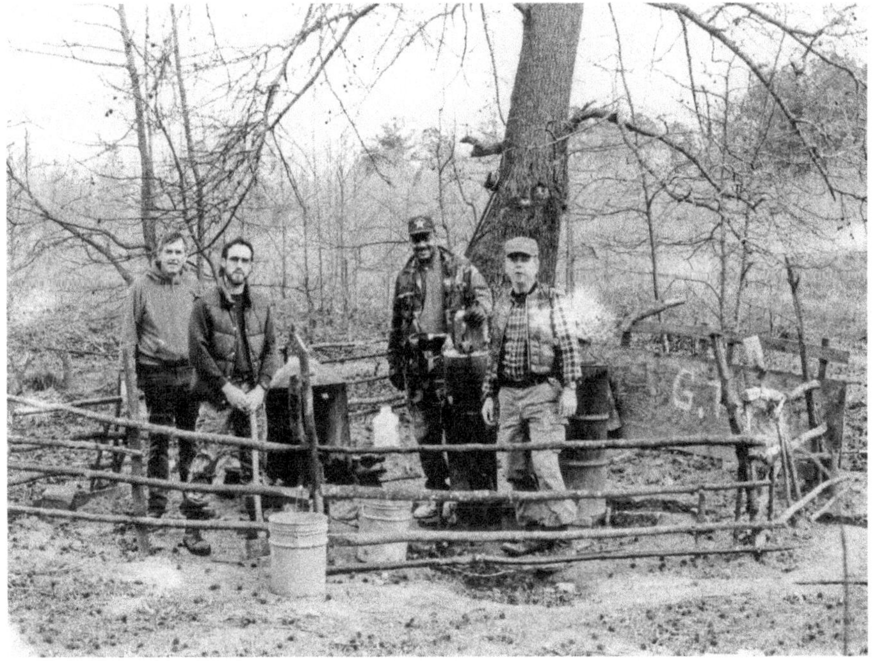

In January 1992, North Carolina ALE officers Bill Williams, Sam Darakgy and Ken Dover with Bertie deputy Donald Cowan raided this still in the San Souci section of Bertie County. *Courtesy of Bertie County Sheriff's Office.*

Opposite, top: All sizes of stills were found all across North Carolina, including jumbo factory stills like this 18,800-mash-capacity one that was found near Murfreesboro in October 1960. In addition to confiscating 6,200 pounds of Peruvian sugar, officers arrested seven still hands at this still. *Courtesy of Joseph Kopka.*

Opposite, bottom: This stovetop still was captured in Archertown in March 1969 by Hertford County ABC officers Livingston Sumner (*left*) and Calvin Pearce (*right*). *Courtesy of Frank Stephenson Jr.*

North Carolina Moonshine

Just about anyone who grew up in the coastal plains region of North Carolina during its moonshine heyday (1930s–1970s) has a personal moonshine story. Many personal moonshine stories came from hunting experiences or just leisurely walks in the woods. At times, particularly on Friday nights, you could literally smell moonshine being made in the coastal plains by riding the backroads. One Sunday morning in December 1957, the minister of a small church in Edgecombe County delivered a fiery sermon to his flock, and at the end of the sermon, he asked the Lord to send the congregation a sign that he had heard them. No sooner had the minister asked the Lord for a sign than two moonshine raiders blew a still that was located about a quarter of a mile behind the church. The dynamite blast shook the church pretty good, prompting the rattled minister to declare, "Lord, we heard you…we didn't need one that loud!"

Some coastal plains fishermen had stories of spotting moonshine operations while fishing. Sometimes, fishermen would observe sugar bags or plastic jugs floating out in the river from small creeks or streams that emptied into the river. Other residents of the coastal plains region recall accidently seeing moonshine being transferred from one vehicle to another or sugar or empty mash barrels being loaded onto trucks from the rear loading docks of local grocery stores late at night.

Some moonshine "sightings" could be quite humorous, as was the case of a report that appeared in the November 1925 issue of the Chowan College student newspaper, the *Chowanian*. The report described how a Chowan College music professor took his class for a walk in the woods near the college and came to a moonshine still that he thought was a molasses mill. The college professor stated, "The substance had a peculiar smell." In the late 1940s, a group of teenage boys living in the Hertford County town of Winton fashioned a huge slingshot out of car tire inner tubes, strung it between two pine trees and used it to hurl huge clods of dirt at boats passing by on the Chowan River. One of the boats they hit was loaded with moonshine, and the dirt clod broke some of the jars of moonshine that the boat was hauling. The maritime bootleggers were furious and started shooting back at the boys. Luckily, none of the boys was hit by the gunfire, but before they fled the scene, the kids had the last word as they lobbed another huge clod of dirt at the boat, knocking one of the bootleggers overboard.

Another coastal plains moonshine discovery happened one warm night in June 1960 at a drive-in theater in an eastern county. Two high school couples were parked on the very back row, enjoying the movie. One of the

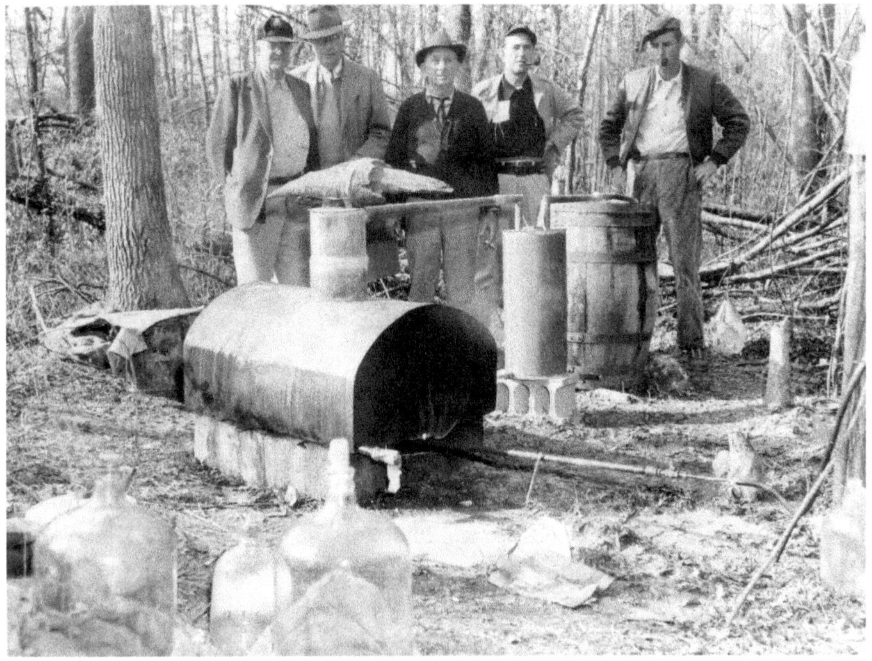

In December 1955, Hertford County moonshine raiders (from left to right) Jack Futrell, Sheriff Charles Parker, Jim Mitchell, Fred Liverman and Livingston Sumner raided this submarine-type still near Murfreesboro. Submarine stills were not commonly found in eastern North Carolina. *Courtesy of Fred Liverman.*

boys caught a whiff of the sweet smell of fermenting mash coming from a small moonshine still that was located on the bank of a creek just behind the drive-in theater. The only access to the drive-in theater was through the front entrance. The next night, the two high school boys returned to the drive-in theater in a florist delivery van belonging to one of the boys' fathers. The boys parked in the very back row, and during the movie, they followed a heavily used path down to the creek, where they found the still. They quietly loaded the still in the delivery van and drove out of the theater unnoticed. The two boys, who were juniors in high school, secretly operated the still for over two years, making and saving enough money for each to pay his way through two years of college. As they were starters on the local high school football team, a linebacker and a fullback, they did not run their still on Friday nights during the football season. Instead, they usually ran it on Thursday nights while listening to late 1950s rock-and-roll music being spun by legendary disc jockey Dick Biondi on WKBW and the Niagara Frontier in Buffalo, New York. The boys were large and rough, had nerves of steel, were not fearful of much of anything and were All-Conference football players during their junior and senior years in high school. Their high school football coach had told his players that he was "looking for boys who on the football field were mean, nasty and ugly." These two boys no doubt were a perfect match for their coach's special qualifications, as both of them were physically tough, rough and could dish it out as well as take it. Both boys had a number of scholarship offers to play football in college but decided not to accept any of the offers.

For over two years, the high school boys sold all the moonshine they could run off to a local bootlegger named Red Horse. Red Horse reportedly supplied North Carolina–made moonshine to shot houses in Washington, D.C., and Baltimore for over thirty years. Red Horse died in an automobile accident when he was hit head-on by a drunk driver in Oxen Hill, Maryland. One of the boys graduated from the University of North Carolina–Chapel Hill with a law degree while the other boy graduated from Virginia Tech with a degree in civil engineering. Each of the boys enjoyed long and successful careers in North Carolina before retiring, one in 2009 and the other in 2011. The fate of the still that they ran for two years in the early 1960s remains a mystery today.

A moonshine story with a totally different twist to it took place in the mid-1950s. Two high school students from Halifax County slipped up on a still operated by a county sheriff. The two boys were undetected and backed off, though they returned the next day and took the still. They set the still up and first ran off seventeen gallons of liquid thunder, of which they sold fourteen gallons and drank the rest. A few weeks later they sold the still back to the sheriff after he had followed them for some days suspecting that they had taken the rig.

There are numerous accounts of high school boys across North Carolina being involved in moonshine one way or another. A number of high school boys made some extra money by hauling loads of moonshine for bootleggers. Many of their loads were hauled to locations in Virginia, Tennessee, South Carolina and Georgia. These boys were taking a huge risk by hauling moonshine, and despite several close calls, none of them ever got caught at it.

A razor-thin close call occurred on the night of November 5, 1957, around 1:00 a.m. during a massive statewide manhunt for Frank Wetzel, a fugitive who reportedly had killed two North Carolina highway patrolmen in Richmond and Lee Counties earlier that day. North Carolina had sealed

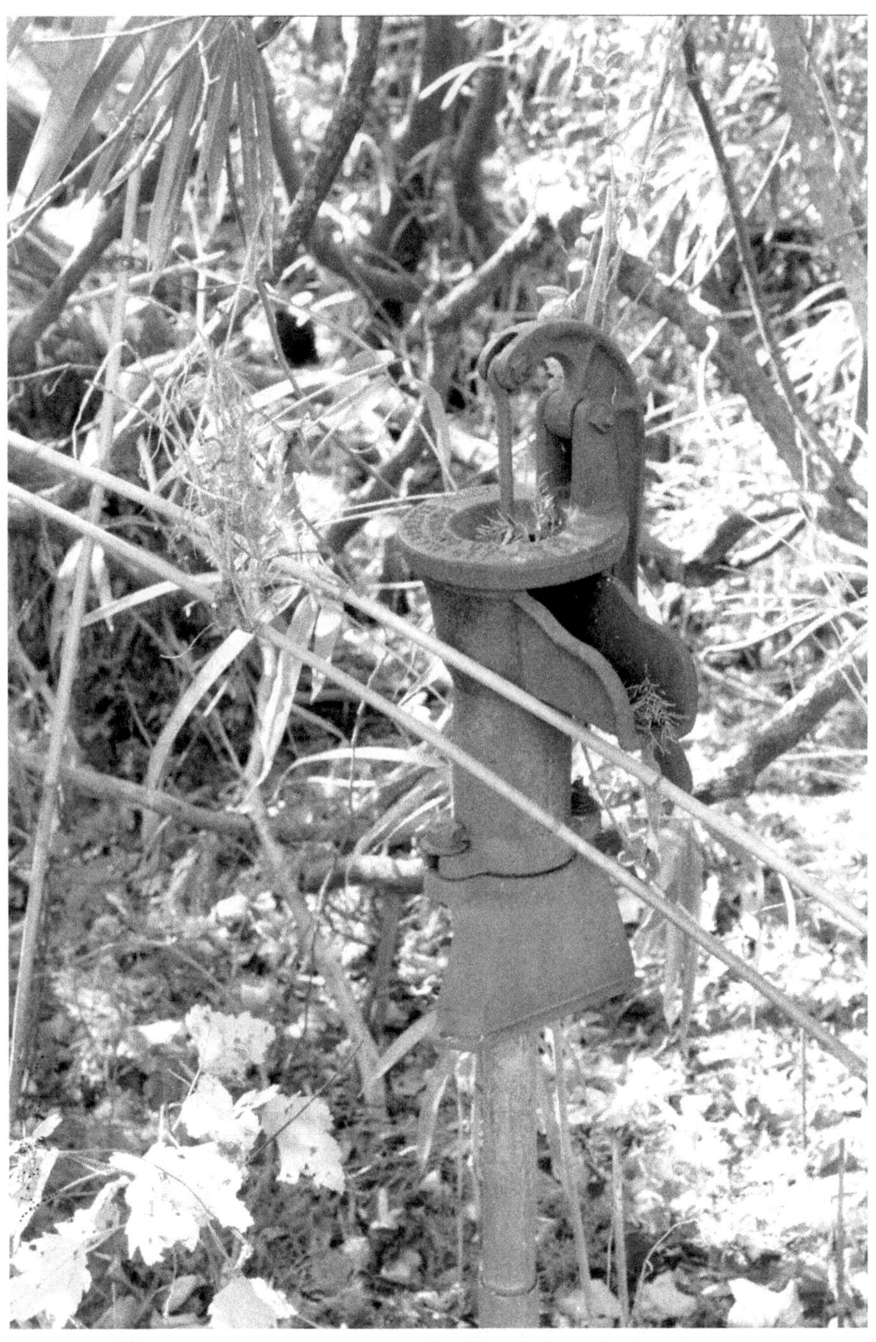

Hand water pumps like the one shown here were among the devices/equipment used to secure water for moonshine stills. *Photograph by Frank Stephenson Jr.*

its borders, and over five hundred officers were on the hunt for the killer. At the same time, a high school moonshine runner was cruising along U.S. 17, north of Elizabeth City heading to Norfolk, Virginia, to deliver a load of moon for a local bootlegger. The high school driver was in a 1955 Chevrolet equipped with a Super Power Pack V-8 engine and extra-heavy-duty rear springs. The moonshine, contained in half-gallon jars, was hidden in the trunk of the car and underneath a hollowed-out rear seat. The moonshine runner had not encountered much traffic and was rolling along at a good clip, seemingly unaware that he was being followed by three police cars running with their lights turned off. All of a sudden, the three cars turned on their headlights, boxed him in and forced his car off the road. The heavily armed law enforcement officers bolted from their vehicles, quickly surrounded the moonshine runner's car and aimed shotguns and high-powered rifles at him. The driver was immediately pulled from the car and angrily confronted by the stone-faced officers. The whole episode ended about as quickly as it had happened as one of the officers recognized the driver. He asked the student why he was out so late. The driver told him that he was heading home from playing a football game earlier that evening. The officer told him to get back in his car and go home. The driver quickly jumped back in his car and hurriedly disappeared down a side road, stopping briefly to regain his composure and ponder just how close he had been to losing his load of juniper juice and landing himself in a huge pile of trouble.

Frank Wetzel, the subject of the massive statewide manhunt, was apprehended several weeks later in Bakersfield, California, by the FBI and extradited to North Carolina. In 1958, he was convicted on two counts of first-degree murder and sentenced to two life terms in prison. In 2012, Frank Wetzel died in Central Prison in Raleigh, North Carolina, at the age of ninety. He was one the state's longest-serving convicts.

Another close call came one night in 1959, when a high school boy picked up a load of moonshine in Rocky Mount to take it to Richmond, Virginia. On his way through Weldon, North Carolina, on U.S. 301, he decided to stop at a local hot dog joint for a quick bite. Unknown to him, two of the fruit jars of moonshine that had been loaded hurriedly in the trunk of his car had cracked, and the rotgut was seeping onto the pavement where he had parked. Luckily, he consumed his hot dogs and drove off before one of the local drunks walked by and noticed liquor on the pavement.

Two years later, in 1961, a Reidsville, North Carolina high school senior was hauling a load of rattlesnake juice up U.S. 29 North to Danville, Virginia, for a local bootlegger when a North Carolina highway patrolman clocked him

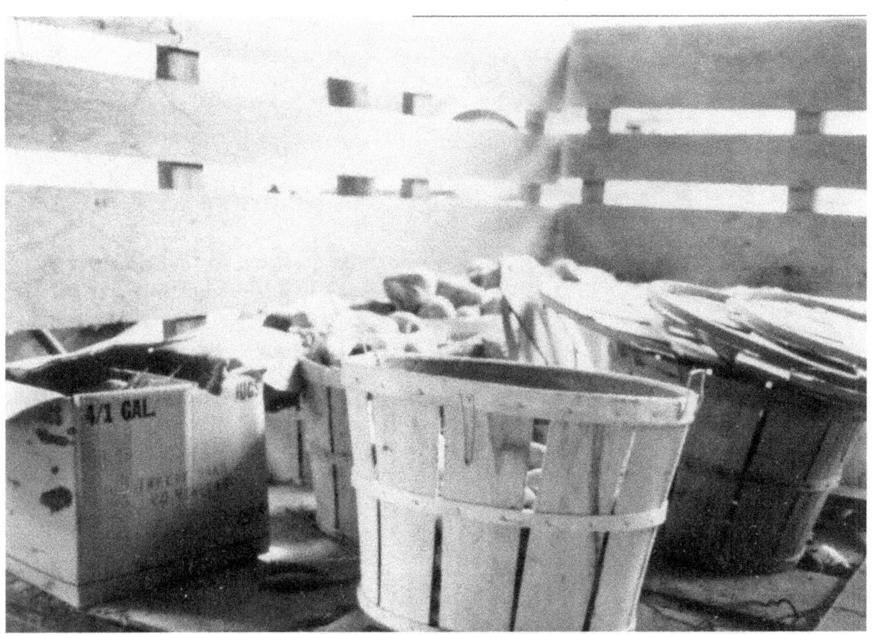

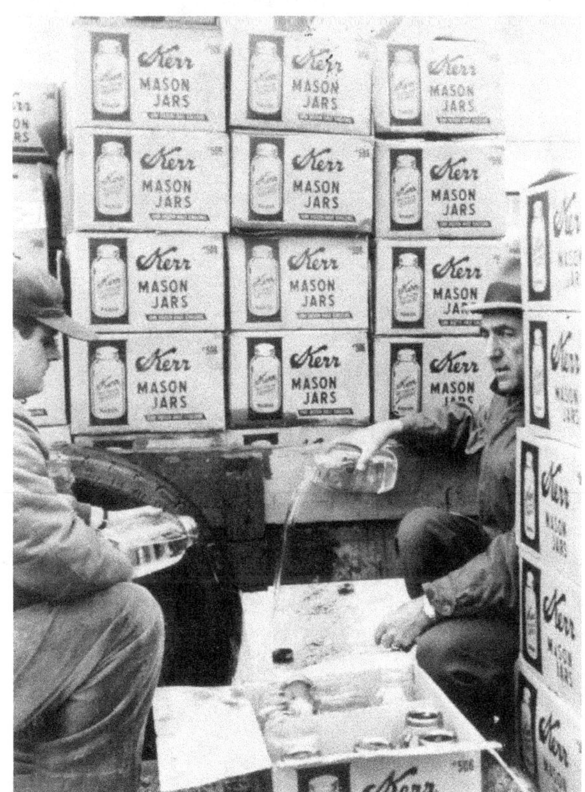

Above: Fruit jars of Gates County moonshine were found hidden in the bottoms of these innocent-looking baskets of sweet potatoes by ATF agent Steve Barrow in 1986. *Courtesy of Steve Barrow.*

Right: Mason jars were a popular moonshine container, as evidenced in this 1960 photograph of jars of moonshine being poured out on a farm near Winton by ATF agent Jack Gaskill (left) and Hertford County deputy Fred Liverman. *Courtesy of Fred Liverman.*

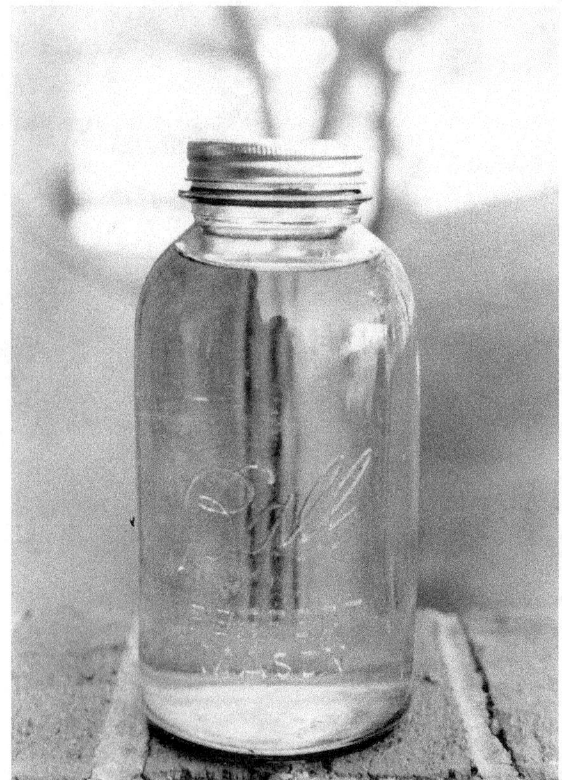

Left: Genuine North Carolina moonshine fruit jar of Hertford County's finest 140-proof stump juice. *Photograph by Frank Stephenson Jr.*

Below: North Carolina moonshine runners utilized all types of automobiles to haul liquor. Two of the more popular vehicles were the 1940 Ford and later the 1949 Ford (shown here) with high-powered engines. This 1949 Ford was a product of a hot-rod garage in Northampton County that specialized in high-speed automotive engines. *Photograph by Frank Stephenson Jr.*

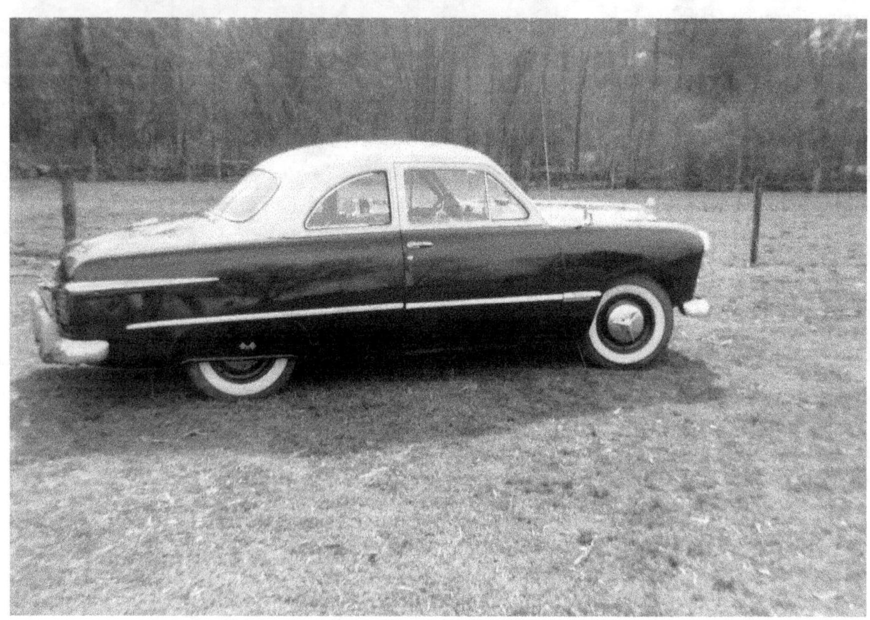

at eighty-nine miles per hour near the small town of Pelham. Fortunately, the high school senior managed to get away when he crossed the North Carolina–Virginia state line—the North Carolina Highway patrolman would not continue the pursuit into Virginia.

While none of the coastal plains region moonshine drivers became famous NASCAR drivers, as did some of the early moonshine drivers in the mountain region, a handful of coastal plain drivers were just as skilled, crafty and evasive. They drove all types of fast cars, but their favorite moonshine-running vehicles were souped-up 1949 Fords with Rocket 88 Olds and Cadillac engines and 1955 Chevrolets. A clandestine auto garage specializing in high-powered moonshine vehicles was located in an isolated wooded area in Northampton County near the North Carolina–Virginia line. This garage was operated for over thirty-five years by a shrewd, large and wily mechanic named Jelly Belly who provided moonshine runners near and far with powerful cars that were almost uncatchable. Jelly Belly died in late 1975, when one of the high-powered engines he was working on blew up and he was struck in the head by a piston.

The three geographic regions of North Carolina each had persons and locations that became famous for being associated one way or another with moonshine. While hundreds of people and locations in the coastal plains region had a history with moonshine over the years, bootlegger Alvin Sawyer of Elizabeth City and the moonshine town of Buffalo City near East Lake in the Alligator River National Wildlife Refuge in Dare County appear to have gained the most notoriety.

Sawyer, a Marine Corps veteran of World War II, became widely known as the Moonshine King of the Great Dismal Swamp for spending most of his life making moonshine in and around one of the most inhospitable places in North Carolina. Although the Great Dismal Swamp was known for its hostile environment, it was a haven for moonshiners and home to numerous liquor stills throughout the years. Buffalo City was a sawmill and logging town where thousands of gallons of rotgut were made from the late 1800s through the Great Depression; at one point, it was known as the Moonshine Capital of North Carolina.

What did Murfreesboro's F. Roy Johnson, a well-known historian, folklorist and publisher, have in common with Elizabeth City's Alvin Sawyer, a famous bootlegger and welder by profession? The unlikely duo spent a considerable amount of time in the Great Dismal Swamp at the same time. Johnson was searching the swamp for Native American and runaway slave artifacts while Sawyer was operating many of his moonshine stills in the swamp. As large an area as the Great Dismal Swamp covers, it would seem almost impossible that Johnson and Sawyer would ever cross paths in the swamp, but in fact, they did, not once but twice. Roy Johnson shared these encounters with his longtime friend Frank Stephenson.

Johnson told Stephenson that his first encounter with Sawyer was when he walked up on Sawyer asleep at his still. At first Sawyer thought Johnson was a moonshine raider, but Johnson assured Sawyer that he was not and that he, Johnson, did not care one way or the other about Sawyer's still. He would not disclose its location. The two totally opposite men pulled up a bucket and talked for several hours about life in the Dismal Swamp before Johnson left. Their second encounter took place a few months later, near the shore of Lake Drummond. Sawyer walked up on Johnson at his campsite. Johnson offered to share some coffee and week-old doughnuts with Sawyer, who took him up on his offer. The two men talked for several hours about folklore, the old way life in the Great Dismal Swamp and Johnson's books before Johnson loaded his camping gear in his canoe, pushed the canoe out in Lake Drummond and paddled off.

Johnson and Sawyer never saw each other again. Johnson died in 1988 while Sawyer, who started making moonshine when he was fifteen years old, died in 2003. In October 2014, the North Carolina Department of Cultural Resources erected a North Carolina Highway Marker in honor of F. Roy Johnson, and at the same time, Alvin Sawyer's reputation as a bootlegger continued to grow and spread; today, he is a celebrity on Elizabeth City's Annual Ghost Walk and is one of North Carolina's most famous bootleggers.

It is interesting to note that for more than twenty-five years of Alvin Sawyer's fifty-plus-year moonshine career, he was constantly being pursued by veteran Pasquotank ABC officer Benny Halstead of Elizabeth City. Halstead, who had a stellar career pursuing moonshiners, is credited with arresting over 1,200 bootleggers, including Sawyer, during his law enforcement career. Halstead arrested Alvin Sawyer a number of times for making moonshine. In their last years, the two men were residents of the same nursing home in Elizabeth City. Sawyer, in an article in the July 1993 issue of *The State* magazine, spoke about the great respect and admiration that he had for his longtime nemesis Benny Halstead, who died in September 1998. Alvin Sawyer died five years later, in August 2003. Both men are buried in Elizabeth City.

Several years before the death of Alvin Sawyer, Frank Stephenson had the opportunity to meet and talk with the retired Great Dismal Swamp bootlegger at the North Carolina Watermelon Festival in Murfreesboro, where Sawyer was selling his miniature stills. Sawyer asked Stephenson about the Johnson man from Murfreesboro whom he had met in the Great Dismal Swamp on two different occasions. Stephenson told Sawyer that he and Johnson were close friends and that he had delivered the eulogy at Roy Johnson's funeral service in October 1988. Sawyer spoke kindly of Johnson and asked about what kind of books Johnson had authored. Stephenson explained that Johnson wrote books mainly on folklore and Native Americans. Alvin Sawyer indicated that he liked books on "Indians" and then told Stephenson that he had seen his book on moonshine, *Carolina Moonshine Raiders*. Sawyer further explained that he personally knew some of the law enforcement officers who were in Stephenson's moonshine book, particularly Benny Halstead, who had chased him for years. Before Sawyer returned to Elizabeth City that day, Stephenson gave him two of Roy Johnson's books on Native Americans and a copy of *Carolina Moonshine Raiders*. Sawyer profusely thanked Stephenson for the books. The Great Dismal Swamp bootlegger and Stephenson never met again.

Today, when you travel along U.S. 64 in Dare County west of Manteo and pass through the section known as East Lake, there are no signs or markers certifying that this is where one of North Carolina's greatest moonshine producing sites, Buffalo City, was located. In the last quarter of the 1800s, a sawmill and logging town was established here on Milltail Creek by the Buffalo Timber Company of New York. The prime purpose of the town was to access the huge supply of timber that was available in the region. The rapid growth of the town brought on by the construction of a hotel, church, store, schoolhouse and company-owned houses resulted in the establishment of a U.S. Post Office there in October 1899. The town's population burgeoned to over three thousand, and at one time, it was the largest town in Dare County. Following the depletion of the region's vast stock of timber and the introduction of the Eighteenth Amendment, Buffalo City began producing moonshine in huge quantities, becoming the Moonshine Capital of North Carolina.

Randall Holmes of Manteo, who grew up in Buffalo City, stated in a January 2016 interview with the authors that at one time, there were over twenty stills running simultaneously in and near Buffalo City. Holmes further explained that most of the whiskey that was produced at Buffalo City was made using rye meal instead of corn and that it was of exceptional quality. According to Holmes, one particular Buffalo City bootlegger would not sell his moonshine immediately after it was run off; instead, he would bury his jugs of finished product in the ground and let it age for thirteen months. Holmes also explained that moonshine from Buffalo City was shipped by boat in huge quantities up and down the eastern seaboard of the United States.

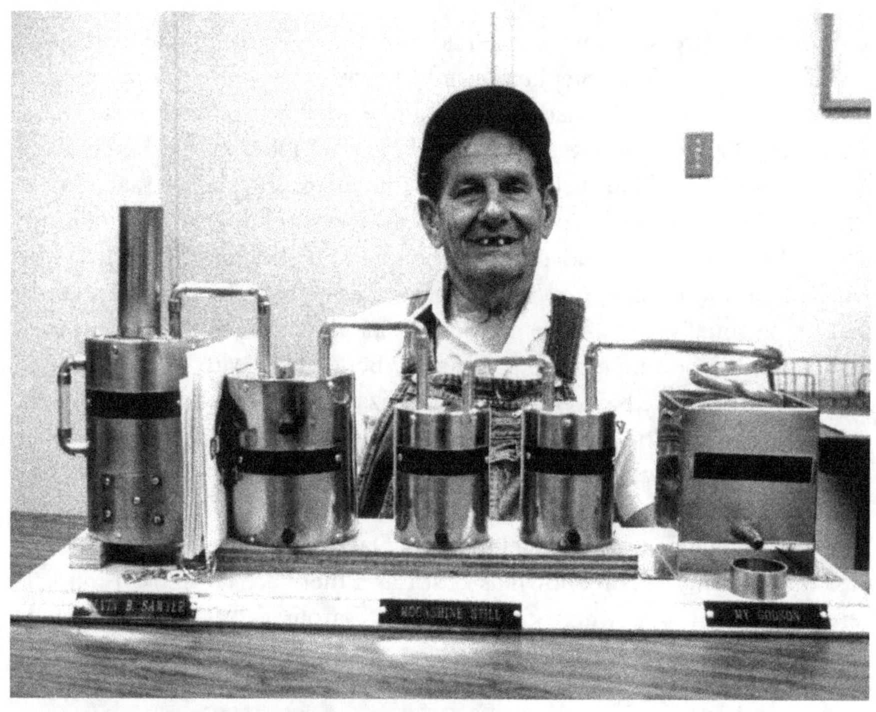

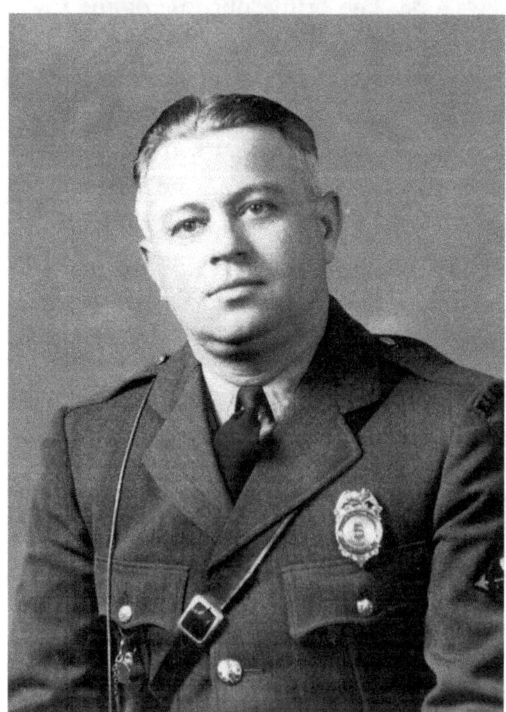

Above: Alvin Sawyer, a master welder and Marine Corps veteran of World War II, spent most of his life making moonshine in the northeastern part of North Carolina. He became known as the "King of Moonshine in the Great Dismal Swamp." *Courtesy of Frank Stephenson Jr.*

Left: Pasquotank ABC officer Benny Halstead of Elizabeth City had over 1,200 moonshine-related arrests during his fifty-plus-year career as a law enforcement officer. *Courtesy of the Halstead family.*

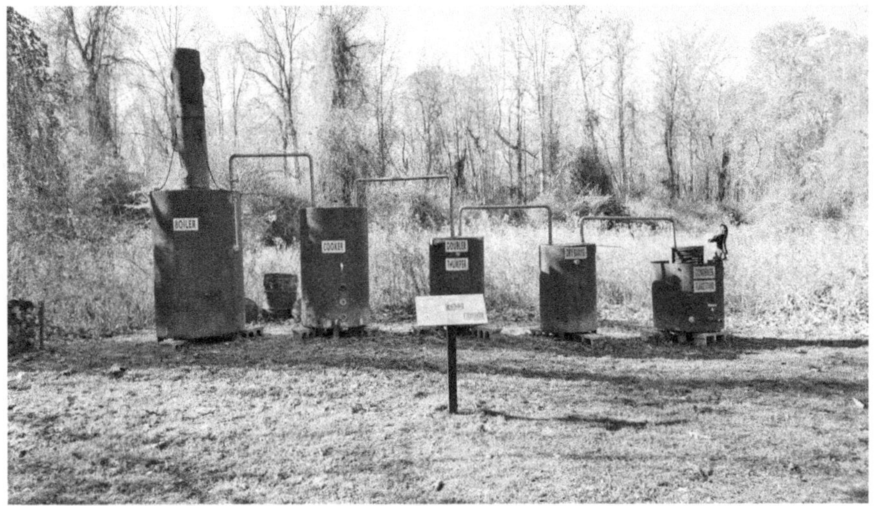

North Carolina's Dismal Swamp State Park in Camden County features this exhibit of stills that were a part of the moonshine legacy of the Great Dismal Swamp. *Photograph by John L. Stephenson.*

Norfolk, Virginia, and points as far north as Boston were serving moonshine made in Buffalo City. By the time World War II broke out, Buffalo City and its moonshine business had died, bringing to a close one of the more colorful chapters in North Carolina's long and illustrious moonshine legacy. Since time and tide wait for no one, the abandoned Buffalo City town site was eventually swallowed up by the thick jungle-like wilderness of Dare County. A few isolated artifacts from life in Buffalo City can probably be kicked up today as one walks along the banks of Milltail Creek.

The *Richmond Times Dispatch* in its December 14, 1928 issue reported on a "big raid conducted in the East Lake section of North Carolina by federal prohibition forces from Richmond, Norfolk and the US Coast Guard at Elizabeth City." The article further stated, "Six complete steam stills, ranging in size from 500 to 800 gallons, in capacity, were seized, along with 50,000 gallons of mash. The stills were operated by twenty horse-power steam boilers with water pumps and modern coils."

It is interesting to note that Frank Cahoon, who was born in the moonshine mecca of East Lake in 1907, served as sheriff of Dare County for thirty-six years. He was a soft-spoken, well-respected man who never carried a weapon or wore a uniform. Sheriff Cahoon, according to his son, Jerry Cahoon, "would call people up who he had a warrant for and convince them to come down to his office to turn themselves in." Jerry said, "I am

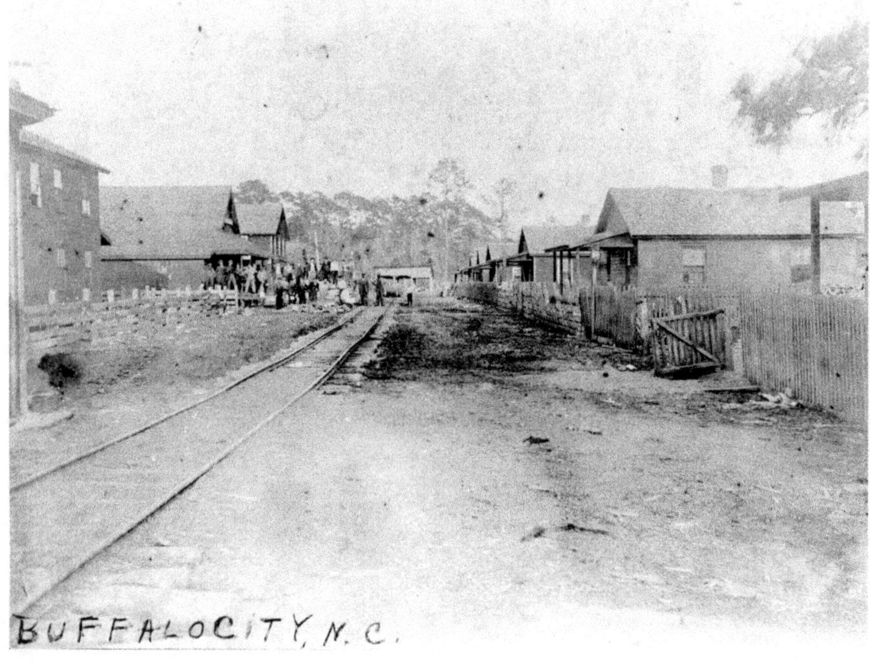

In the early nineteenth century, Buffalo City in Dare County was known as the "Moonshine Capital of the World." This is a circa 1915 view of its Main Street. *Courtesy of the Outer Banks History Center, Manteo, North Carolina.*

almost sure he never fired his weapon at anyone during his years as sheriff of Dare County."

A little farther down the North Carolina coast, above Wilmington in Pender County, one of the largest stills ever found in the state was raided by federal moonshine raiders on October 11, 1973, at Malpass Corner near the small town of Magnolia. Federal agent Ralph Ellis, who headed the raid, stated, "The massive still had a mash capacity of nearly 17,300 gallons and was capable of producing over one million dollars of moonshine a year." Ellis further stated, "It was one of the most supplicated operations I had ever seen, probably costing over $20,000 to build, and it probably operated twenty-four hours a day." Five bootleggers were arrested at the site while another was arrested in New York City trying to deliver a load of moonshine. One of the men who was arrested at the still was a vice-principal of a local school system; another was from Rougemont in Durham County, and two were from Rocky Mount and Bailey in Nash County. When news of the raid rapidly spread throughout the region, thousands of curious folks flocked to the site to take a look at the behemoth still. Most of the visitors

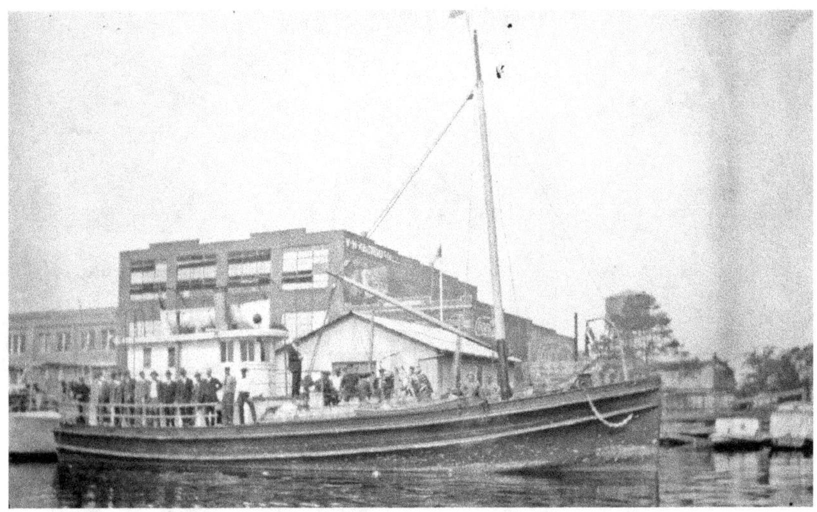

In December 1928, federal Prohibition forces from Richmond and Norfolk, Virginia, conducted a moonshine raid by boat at East Lake/Buffalo City in Dare County. *Courtesy of Outer Banks History Center, Manteo, North Carolina.*

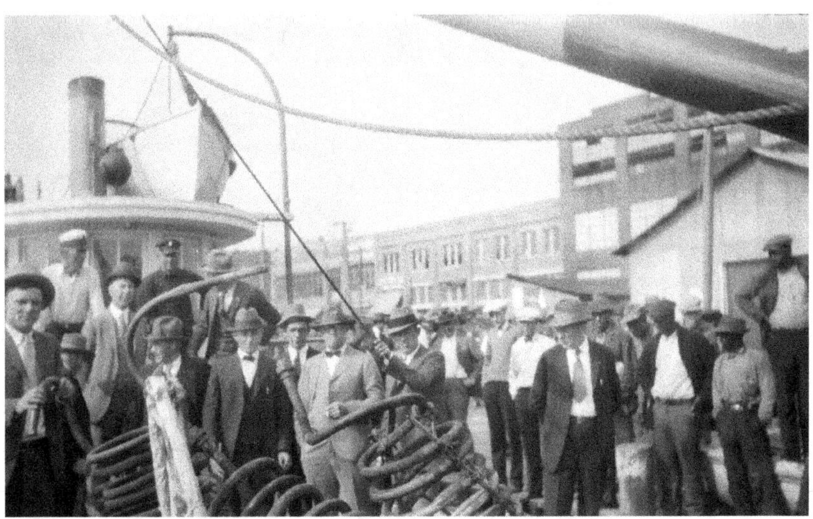

Federal moonshine raiders on the boat raid. *Courtesy of Outer Banks History Center, Manteo, North Carolina.*

could not believe that such a thing like that was in operation right under their noses. Two days later, an Explosive Ordnance Demolition Unit from Camp Lejeune, North Carolina, destroyed the moonshine factory in one massive explosion.

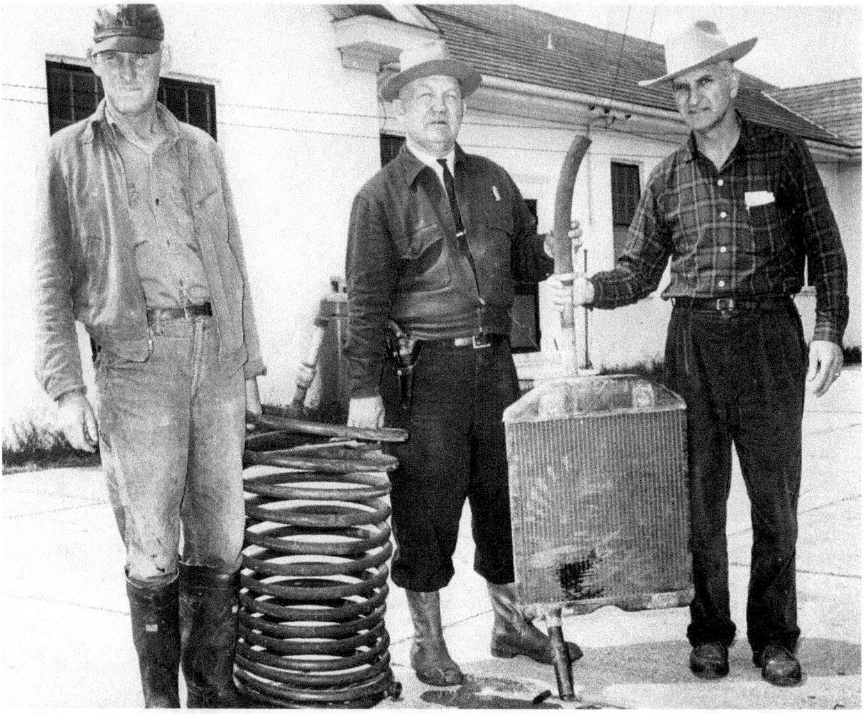

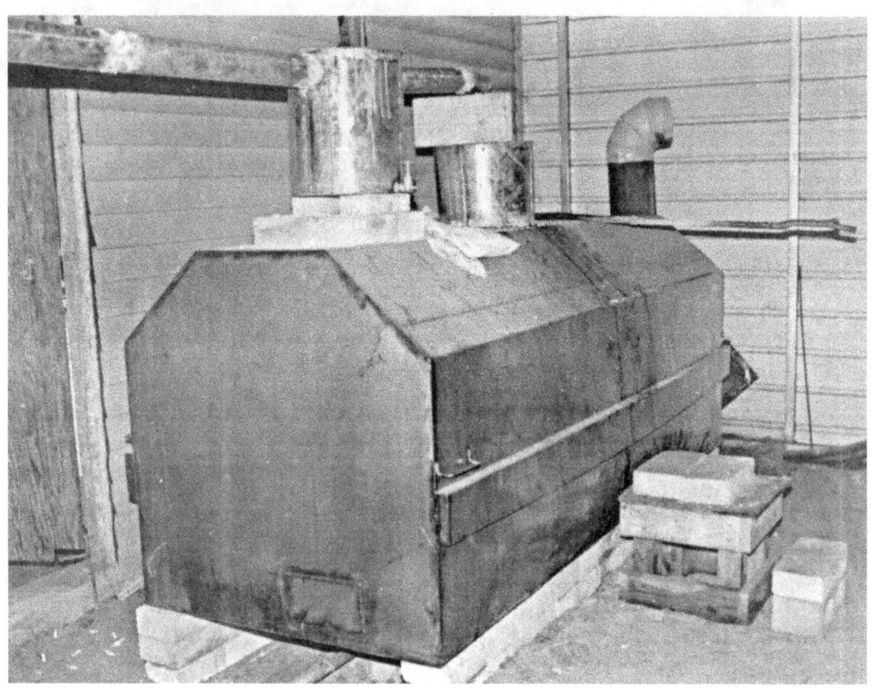

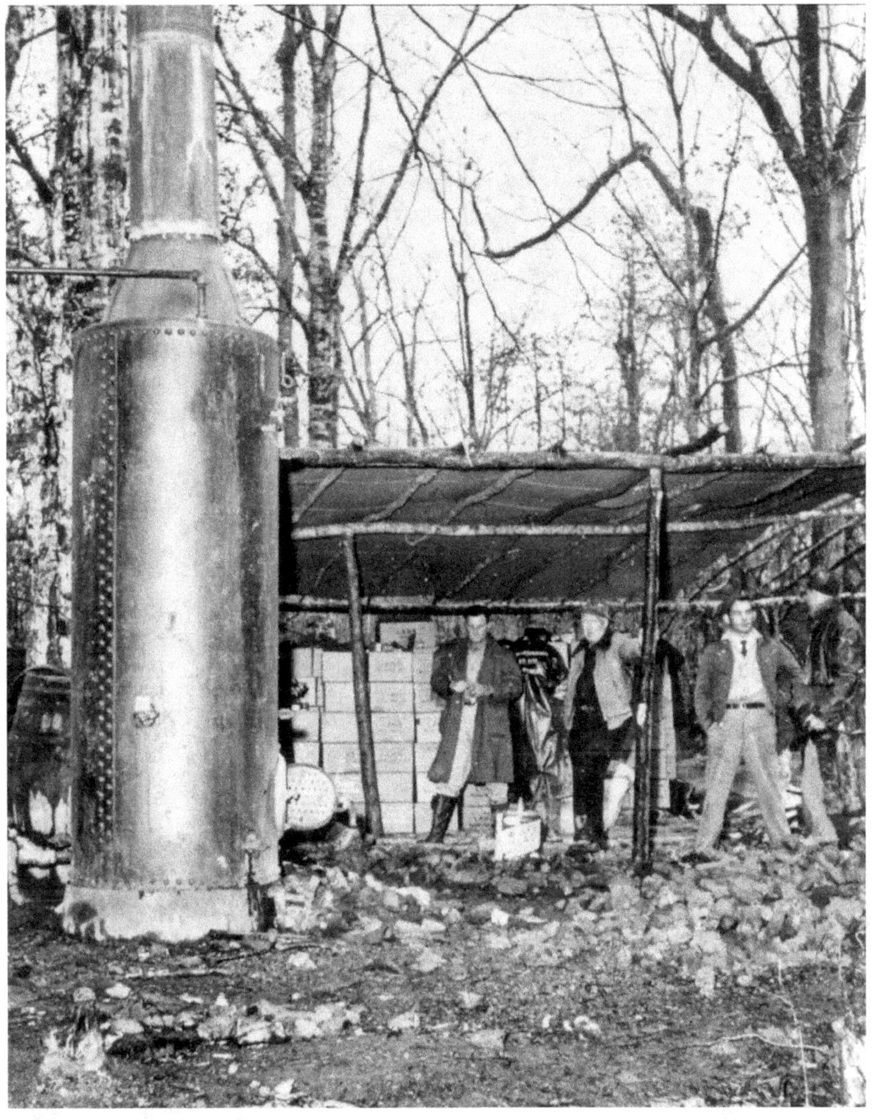

Jumbo stills—such as this one, which was raided near Cofield in Hertford County on February 17, 1956, by ATF and local moonshine raiders—were found all across North Carolina. *Courtesy of Fred Liverman.*

Opposite, top: *From left to right*: Deputy Sheriff Clarence Hassell, Manteo police chief Chester Mitchell and Sheriff Frank Cahoon with the remains of a still they raided in Kitty Hawk in the early 1960s. *Courtesy of the Outer Banks History Center, Manteo, North Carolina.*

Opposite, bottom: This is the stainless steel cooker to a huge still that was raided in March 1999 in the Eure section of Gates County by local and state moonshine raiders. *Courtesy of Gates County sheriff Ed Webb.*

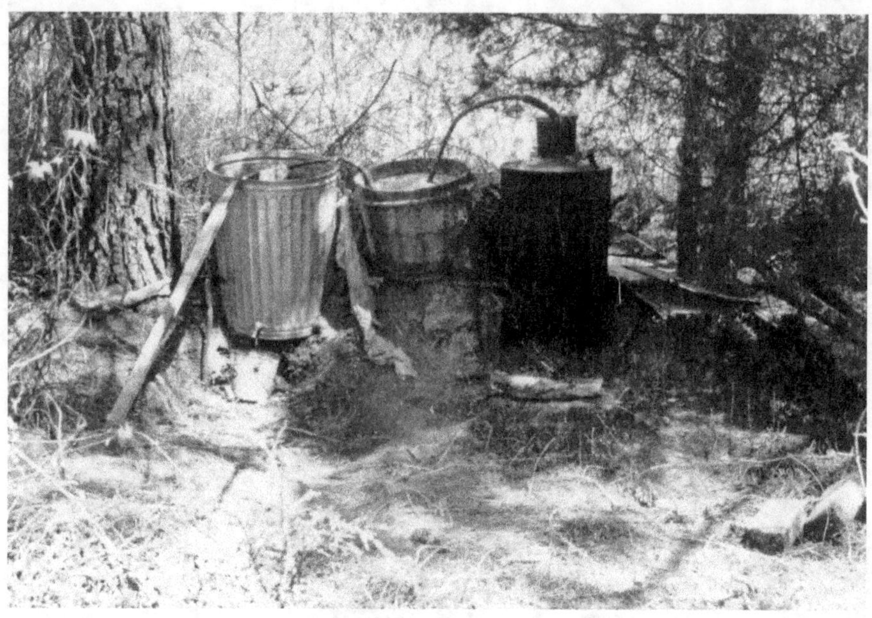

Improvisation was the keyword for this bootlegger; he used an old wash tub, a garbage can and other odd pieces to cobble together this junk still. Northampton County moonshine raider Earl Outland hit this still on April 24, 1971, near Henrico. *Courtesy of Earl Outland*

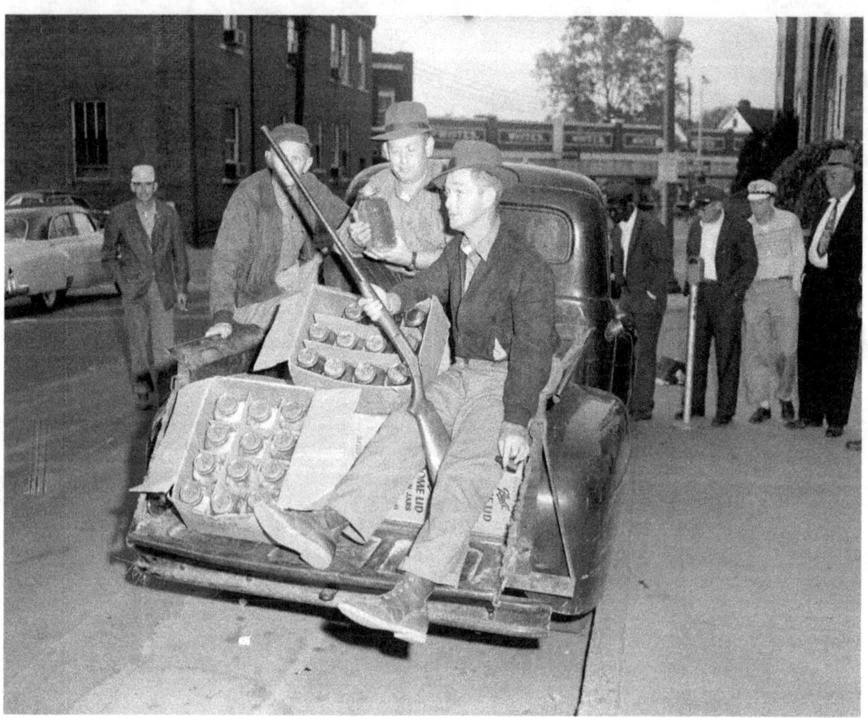

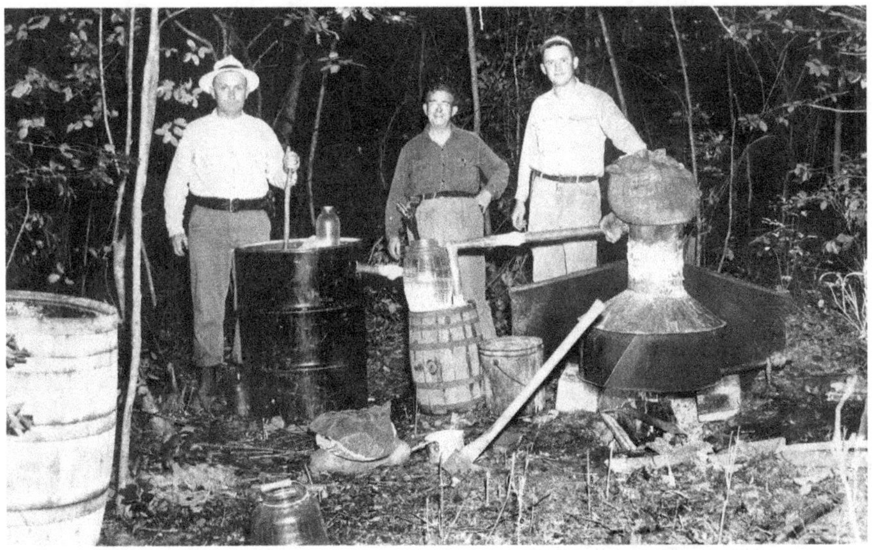

Liquor still discovered in Greene County, North Carolina, in the late 1940s; at left is Deputy Sheriff Walter L. Heads (1908–1993); at center is the sheriff. *Courtesy of State Archives of North Carolina.*

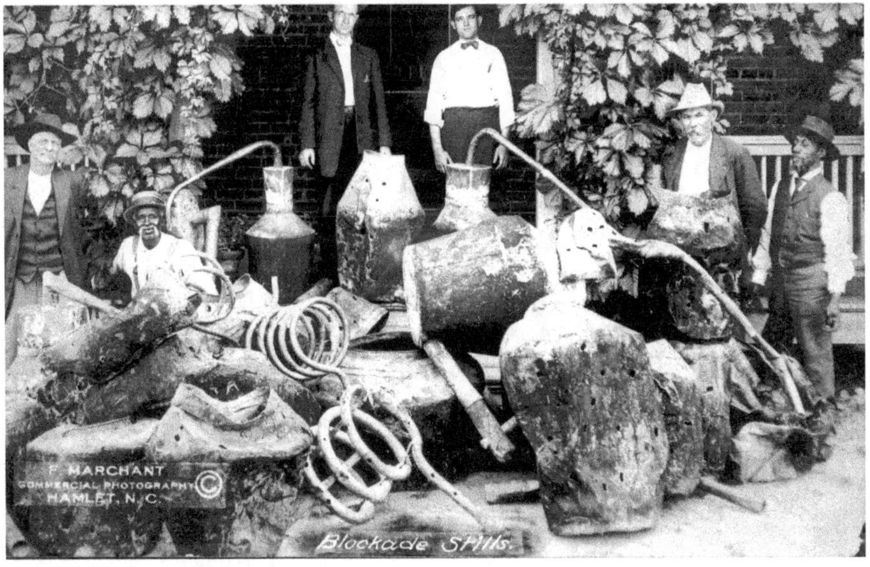

Blockade Stills, postcard by Frank Marchant, Hamlet, North Carolina, circa 1909. *Courtesy of State Archives of North Carolina.*

Opposite, bottom: Pitt County moonshine raiders (from left to right) H.B. Lilly, J.M. Ward and W.M. Taylor in the back of a truck with 122 gallons of bootleg liquor they seized following a high-speed chase. *Courtesy of the* Daily Reflector *Image Collection, J.Y. Joyner Library, East Carolina University, http://digital.lib.ecu.edu/2602.*

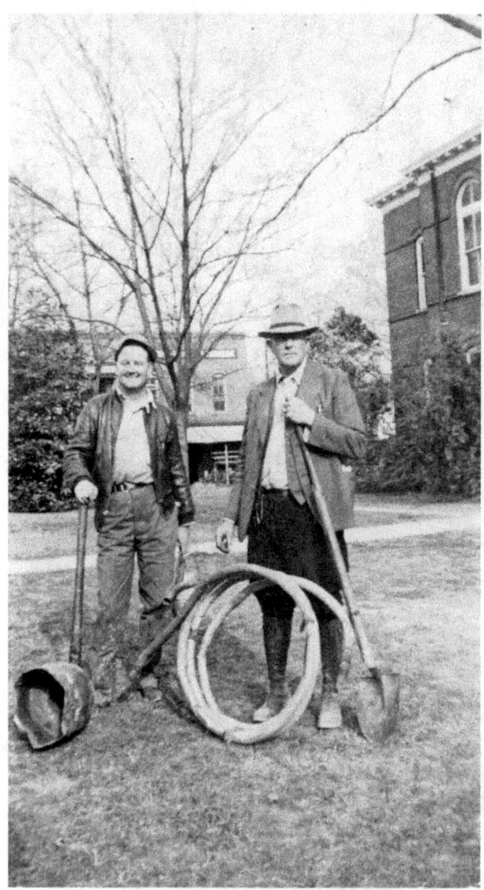

Left: Onslow County moonshining, circa 1940s, in the North Carolina Photographic Collection #P0001. *Courtesy of North Carolina Collection Photographic Archives, the Wilson Library, University of North Carolina–Chapel Hill.*

Below: North Carolina Alcohol Law Enforcement (ALE) officer Gail Jackson at a still that ALE raided in Bertie County on February 27, 1988. *Courtesy of North Carolina Alcohol Law Enforcement Office, Edenton, NC.*

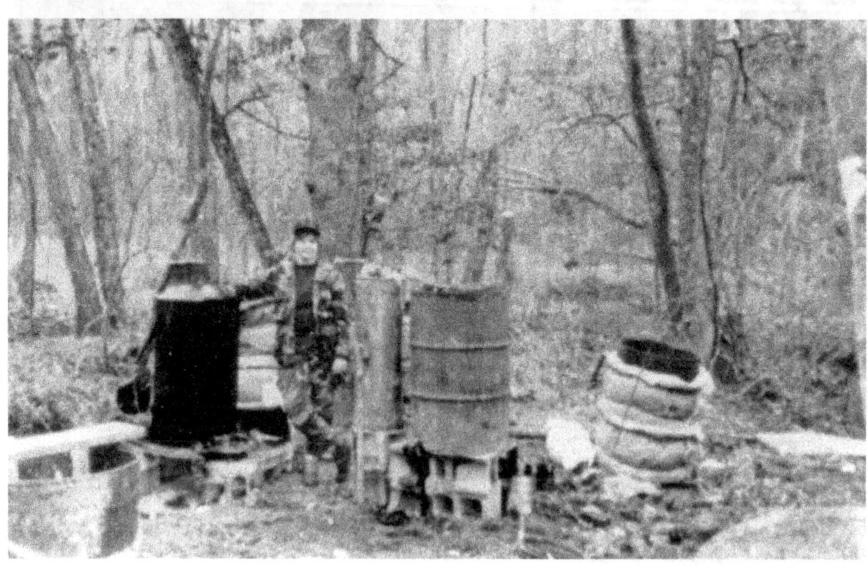

Right, top: Halifax County ABC officer Garland Bunting and ATF agent Edward Garrison at a still that they had raided in Northampton County. *Courtesy of Edward Garrison.*

Right, bottom: Calvin Pearce at still in Northampton County, 1960s. *Courtesy of Edward Garrison.*

Below: ATF raided this still in Camden County in the 1970s. Moses Hershaw is the ATF agent wearing the firearm. *Courtesy of Steve Barrow.*

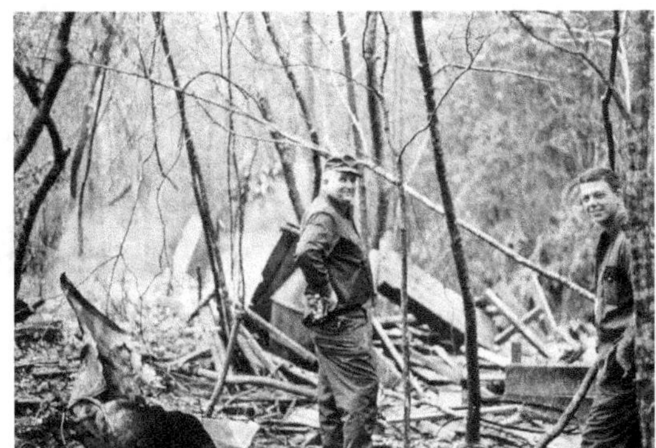

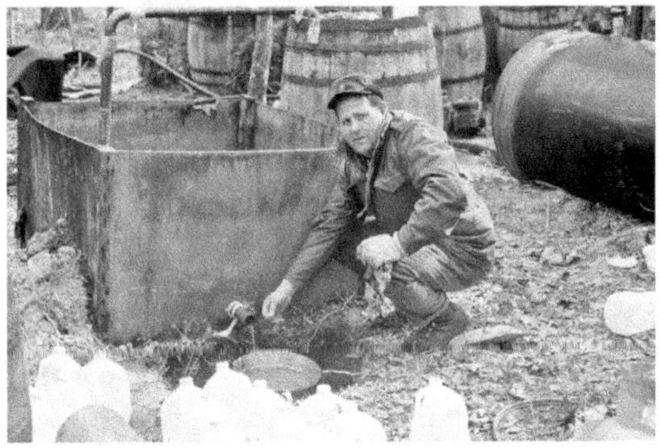

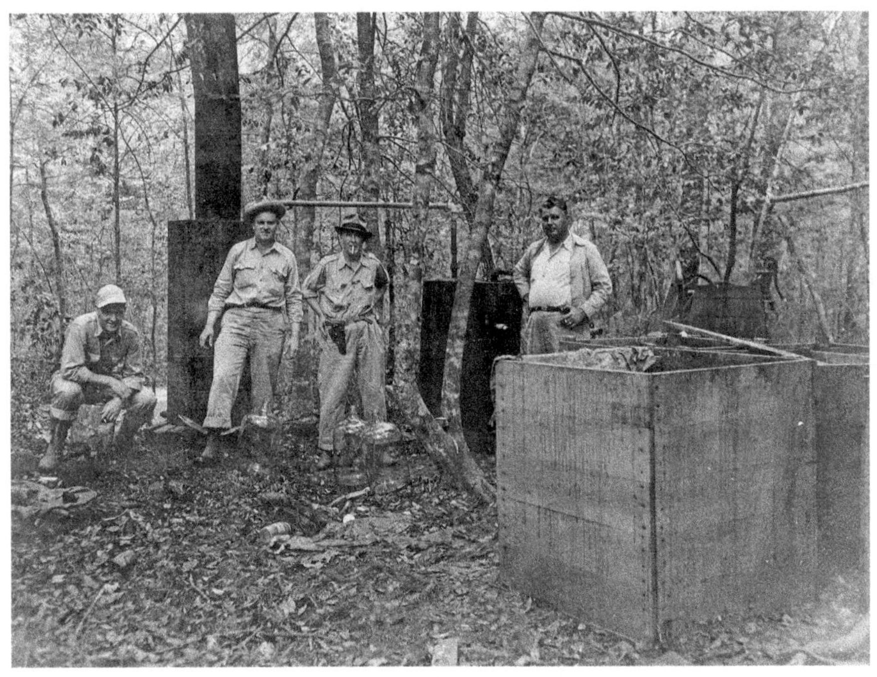

Chapter 2

CENTRAL REGION

Rolling Hills of Rotgut

North Carolina's most populous section is the central region, which extends from Warren County in the northeast part of the region to Cleveland County in the southwestern corner. While moonshine was made in huge quantities all across the central region of North Carolina, the counties of Harnett and Johnston head the list of top bootleg-producing counties in the region. When the topic of who made the most moonshine in the central region is discussed, Joshua Percy Flowers of Johnston County always tops the list. There is a very good reason for this. Percy Flowers is perhaps best known as North Carolina's most famous bootlegger—a standout, even in a state that was home to Junior Johnson and Marvin "Popcorn" Sutton. Percy Flowers's web of notoriety was unprecedented, legendary and far reaching. This fact seems to be verified by a huge amount of publicity, including a lengthy article by John Kobler titled "King of the Moonshiners" that appeared in the August 2, 1958 issue of the *Saturday Evening Post*. The article chronicles Percy Flowers's long and extensive history with moonshine. The article also details his benevolent side as a staunch pillar of his church and community, particularly his willingness to help those in need and to stand by those who helped him but ran into legal difficulty in doing so.

Frank Stephenson Jr. had an opportunity to personally meet Flowers in 1964, when he, Stephenson, was a student at North Carolina State University in Raleigh, North Carolina. Stephenson had a part-time job with the State of North Carolina Department of Archives and History, and one of his co-workers was Maxie Wall, who lived in the same Johnston County community as Percy Flowers and was lifelong friends with him. The name of Percy Flowers was well known all across North Carolina, and Stephenson found it interesting when he learned that Wall and Percy Flowers were neighbors. Wall asked Stephenson if he would like to meet Percy Flowers one day at his store on NC 42 near Clayton, and Stephenson said he would. Wall cautioned that if Percy Flowers offered him anything, such as a soda or snacks, to not turn it down because if he did, Percy would be offended and would not have anything else to do with him. Frank tells the story this way:

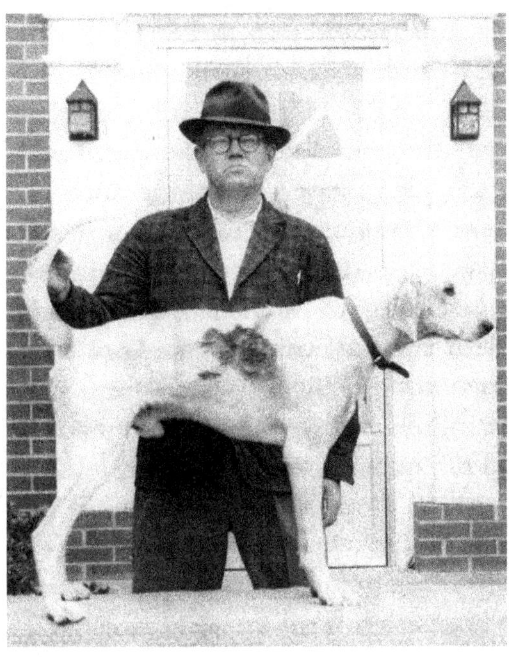

Few North Carolina moonshiners ever achieved the level of notoriety of Johnston County's Percy Flowers. Flowers, whose moonshine empire and web extended far beyond North Carolina, became known as the "King of the Moonshiners" in an article by John Kobler in the August 2, 1958 issue of the *Saturday Evening Post. Courtesy of Perry D. Sullivan.*

ONE WEDNESDAY AFTERNOON, I drove from Raleigh to Mrs. Wall's home near Clayton, and she drove me over to the Percy Flowers store on NC 42. As a senior in college, there I stood in front of the store about to meet North Carolina's most famous moonshiner and really did not know what to expect. I was not afraid or hesitant, as I knew that my friend Maxie Wall would not take me to a place where we would be in danger. When we entered the store, I saw Mr. Flowers sitting in a heavy rocking chair flanked by two men who I assume were his personal bodyguards. Mr. Flowers who was a fairly large man and his two bodyguards gave me sharp, steel-cutting glares as Mrs. Wall and I approached them. Mrs. Wall introduced me to Mr. Flowers, who shook hands hard with me as he stared me right straight in the face without cracking a smile. "It is a pleasure to meet you, sir. How are you doing Mr. Flowers?" I politely asked as I noticed two more stone-faced men watching us like hawks from behind a slightly ajar storage room door.

"Not doing too bad," Mr. Flowers replied as he motioned for Mrs. Wall and I to have a seat in two hard straight-back chairs that were between him and a large potbelly stove.

"I would like to thank Mrs. Wall for taking the time to bring me over here to meet you, sir," I said as Mrs. Wall and I took a seat in the wooden chairs.

Mr. Flowers cleared his throat, "Why did you want to meet me?"

Before I could answer his question, Mrs. Wall said, "He is a student at State and works with me in the state records center, and I think he is a lot like us—comes from good hardworking country folks."

"Where are you from boy?" Mr. Flowers nodded. "Your accent tells me that you are not from around here."

"No, sir, I grew up on a farm just north of Murfreesboro in Hertford County up in the northeast part of the state, close to Virginia," I replied.

Mr. Flowers stroked his chin, "Hertford County…that's Chowan River country up there, around Ahoskie, Winton and Cofield?"

"Yes, sir, I know where all those places are," I replied. "I have been on the Chowan River many times."

"I've taken my dogs and gone foxhunting up that way a few times. Got some mighty good folks up that way," Mr. Flowers noted.

Mr. Flowers did offer Mrs. Wall and me soft drinks and some crackers, which we graciously accepted. After about an hour, Mrs. Wall and I thanked Mr. Flowers for the hospitably, and we loaded back in her car. As we drove off, I looked back at the Flowers store on Highway 42 and pondered what had just happened. I had met North Carolina's most famous bootlegger, whose graciousness and demeanor were in total contrast to his famous moonshine reputation. We drove back to Mrs. Wall's home, where I thanked her for taking me to meet the King of North Carolina Moonshine.

Echoes of the huge moonshine empire and legacy of Percy Flowers can still be heard across North Carolina today in the form of numerous stories and accounts of various events that supposedly happened during the Percy Flowers years. One such story involved two bird hunters from Raleigh who decided to go bird hunting south of Raleigh on a farm in Johnston County not far from the Percy Flowers store on Highway 42. One of the hunters had been hunting on the farm previously and had not had any earlier problems gaining access to the farm. But it was a different story on this day. When they arrived at the farm, they were met at the locked gate by two large, armed stone-faced men who told them, "Boys, there ain't no birds on this farm today. You best get back in your car there and leave now." The two thwarted bird hunters heeded the no-nonsense warning from the two stone-faced sentinels.

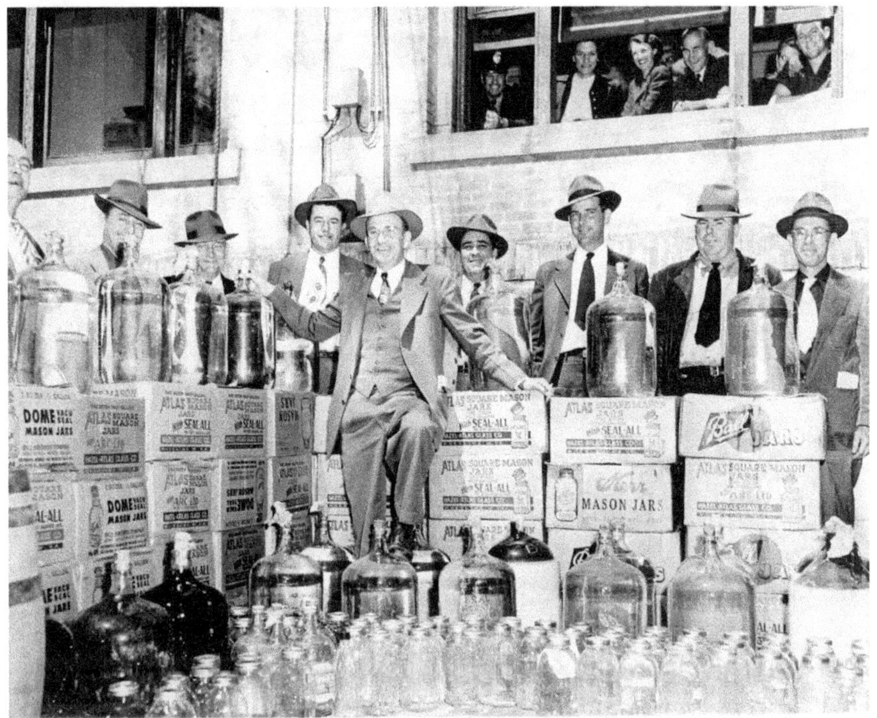

A group of raiders poses with confiscated illegal liquor outside Johnston County Courthouse in 1951. *From left to right*: Roy D. Hinton, jailer; J.T. Smith; Hugh Lamb; unidentified; Barney Henry, sheriff; Alvin Narron; Massengill; Ernie Beasley; and unidentified. *Courtesy of the State Archives of North Carolina.*

A former moonshine raider recently recalled when tractor-trailer trucks would come down to Johnston County from Philadelphia, Baltimore, Washington and other northern cities and return fully loaded with Percy Flowers moonshine. A retired Wake County moonshine raider passed along a story to Stephenson about one of his next-door neighbors who supposedly made his living as a lightning rod salesman. He told Stephenson, "My neighbor's real job was as a likker hauler for Percy Flowers and the lightning rod salesman thing was a perfect cover because he was always on the road." He shook his head negatively and continued:

> *Makes you wonder doesn't it? I mean my neighbor, he was a great family man with a nice wife and four kids, Sunday school superintendent, church deacon, a Mason and a member of the Kiwanis Club. Who would have ever thought he was a likker hauler? Nobody probably would have ever*

WANTED

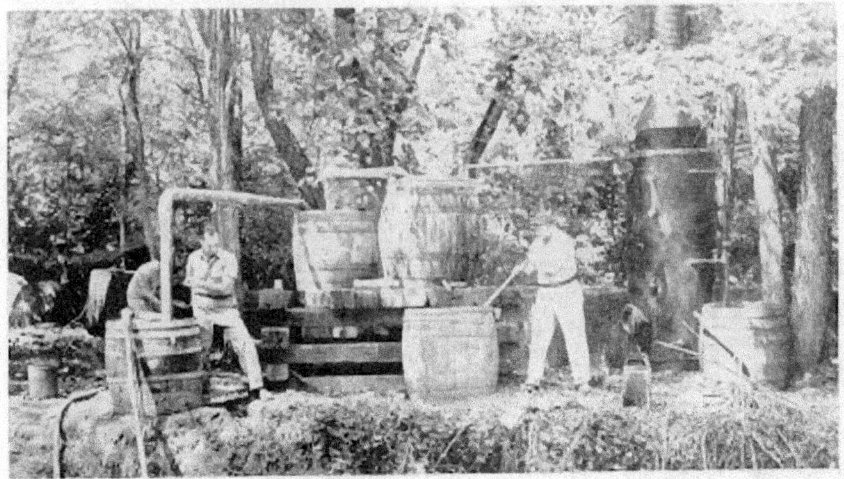

information from **YOU** the taxpayer on the locations of

BOOTLEG STILLS

Moonshine stills in your locality like that pictured above, are robbing you of many thousands of dollars in Federal and State liquor taxes. Help your Government by reporting them, by mail or phone, to

ALCOHOL AND TOBACCO TAX DIVISION, INTERNAL REVENUE SERVICE

All communications held strictly confidential

This poster was one of the weapons that ATF used to fight moonshine in North Carolina. *Courtesy of Johnny Binkley.*

> *found out about his other work if it hadn't been for that wreck he got in up there in Washington, D.C., with that truck load of likker when one of them drunks up there ran into him head on.*

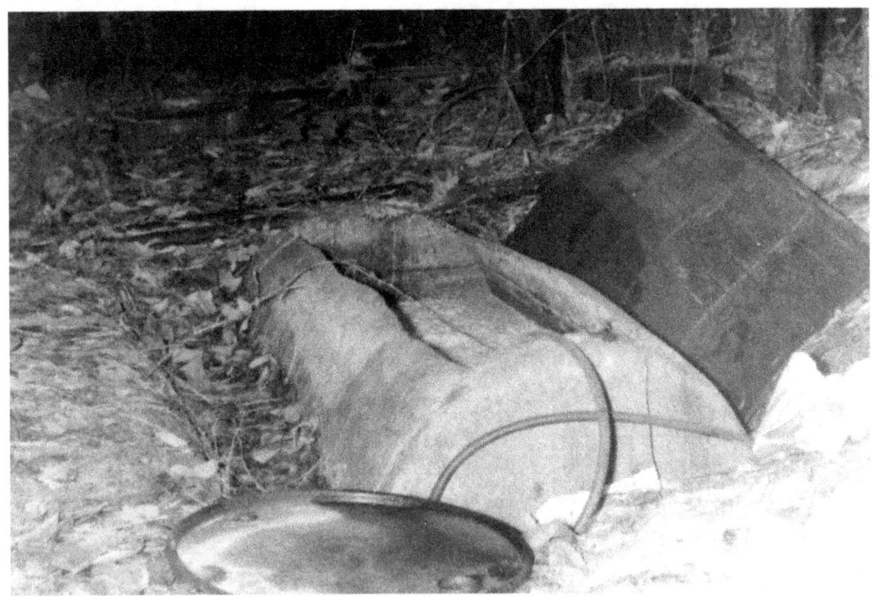

This unusual still was found by Gates County moonshine raiders near Somerton Creek in June 1968. Two bootleggers from Suffolk, Virginia, who were asleep nearby in a two-man Boy Scout tent were arrested. *Courtesy of Calvin Pearce.*

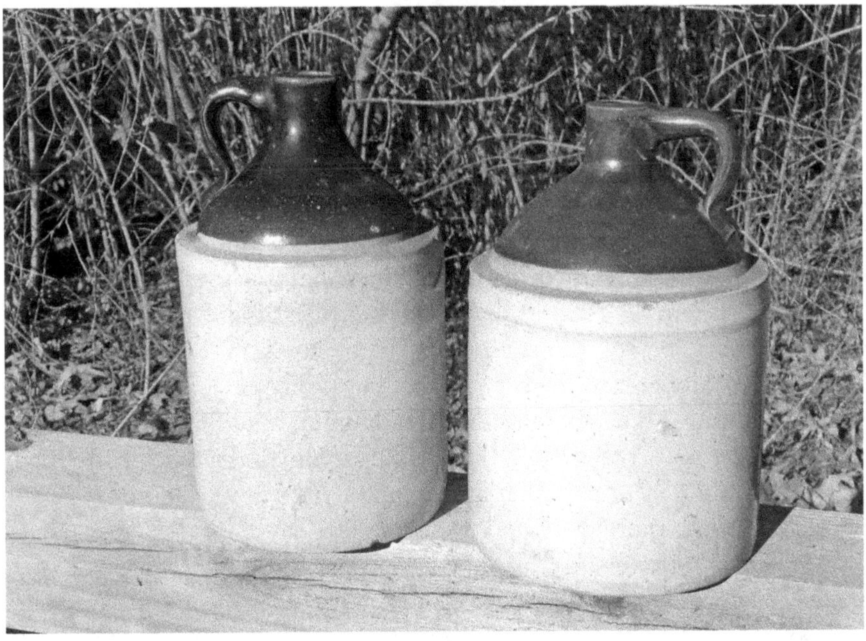

These moonshine jugs were seized by Hertford County deputy Frank Stephenson Sr. and his son Frank Stephenson Jr. on a raid near St. Johns. *Photograph by Frank Stephenson Jr.*

Fascination with Percy Flowers continues today. In 2013, well after Flowers's death in 1982, the book *Lost Flowers* was published by Perry D. Sullivan, one of the sons of Percy Flowers. In the January–February 2015 issue of *Street Scape* magazine, an article about Percy Flowers titled "King of Moonshine" was published.

While the moonshine news in the central region of North Carolina was dominated for many years by the moonshine empire of Percy Flowers of Johnston County and later by Doug Ross of Franklin County, there was a heavy illegal liquor-distilling business all across the region. Harnett County, located to the south of Johnston County, was a major producer of bootleg for years, and some of its bootleggers took their moonshine-making skills and set up shop in other areas of the state. In March 1999, a huge stainless steel still was discovered in the Eure community of Gates County, and two Harnett county bootleggers were arrested for running it. A Gates County water bill that was found on a moonshine raid in Harnett County led to the discovery of the Eure factory still. Another, earlier bust occurred in October 1960, when ATF and regional moonshine raiders hit a factory still near Murfreesboro in Hertford County that was being operated by bootleggers from such central North Carolina places as Durham, Bahama and Rougemont in Durham County. Six thousand pounds of Peruvian sugar and over 120 barrels of mash were found at the still site. Seven still hands who lived in a large tent at the site were arrested. One of the still hands was from Nashville in Nash County.

The Wake Forest Historical Museum has a small undated article that describes an isolated section of the county known as the "Hurricane," where moonshine was produced for many years. The section apparently derived its name from when a strong hurricane roared through the area, producing heavy damage but not destroying its prolific moonshine capability.

In the February 2, 1952 issue of *The State* magazine, writer Penn Gray chronicled the story of the still-busting high sheriff of Robeson County, Malcolm G. McLeod, who when sworn in "promised to get the stills in Robeson County." The six-foot-three, 260-pound moonshine raider whose campaign slogan was "Big Man, Big Job" apparently was a man of his word. The article went on to state that at the end of his first year in office, 1950, Sheriff McLeod reported, "I got 734 stills in 364 days."

"My father told me that his department averaged destroying one and a half stills per day for the first eleven years he was in office," Malcolm McLeod Jr. explained. Sheriff McLeod was in office during some of the county's most contentious times, 1950 to 1978.

In March 1968, the quiet and peaceful central North Carolina county of Cabarrus was rocked with the discovery of one of the largest and most sophisticated and elaborate stills ever seized in the state. Following weeks of investigation, a massive, underground moonshine factory was found near the community of Midland and apparently had been in operation for some time. The complex still was housed in an underground chamber 12 feet wide and 118 feet long. The only entrance to the still was through a trapdoor that was in the floor of an old barn full of hay standing over the still site. The still site was so well disguised that a search of the property several years earlier had failed to reveal any clues of its existence. The still's twelve giant tanks had a mash capacity of nearly thirteen thousand gallons and could produce over six hundred gallons of rotgut daily. The underground chamber also housed thousands of quart jars and hundreds of pounds of sugar and yeast. When the ATF agents, led by special investigator Bob Martin, hit the site, they found over seven hundred gallons of moonshine and over seven thousand gallons of mash ready to be cooked. Two men, one of whom was from Wilkes County, were arrested at the still. A third bootlegger managed to escape and was never arrested. Investigators believed that the owner of the still made over $1 million during its seven years of operation. Furthermore, investigators estimated that the cost to construct the still was over $70,000.

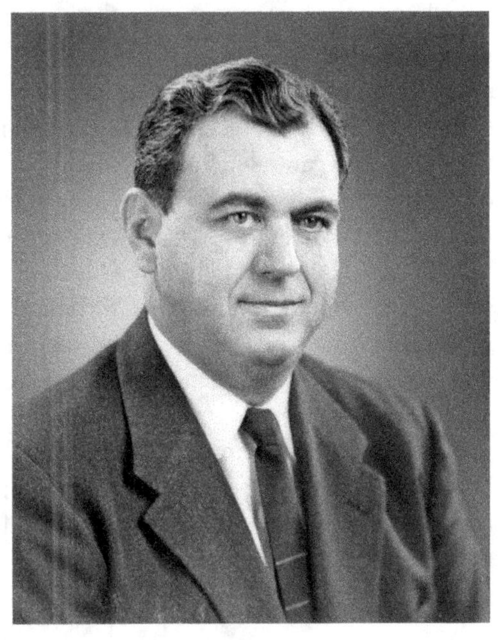

Sheriff Malcolm McLeod. *Courtesy of Malcolm McLeod Jr.*

When news broke of the discovery of the moonshine factory, thousands of people from the region flocked to the area to view it, which created huge traffic jams at times. ATF contracted with Manuel Kiser of Kiser Salvage Company in Concord, North Carolina, to remove the massive distillery. It took Kiser Salvage Company's crews two full days to disable, dismantle and remove the still from its original location to the company's salvage yard on heavily traveled U.S. 29. Curious folks continued to view the remains of the giant still at the Kiser salvage yard on U.S. 29, causing serious traffic jams.

When Kiser Salvage Company completed the job of removing the big Concord still, Manuel Kiser probably had no idea that ATF would contract with him four years later, in 1972, to remove an even larger moonshine factory of the same design. The second massive moonshine factory was located over three hundred miles from the first, in the Merry Hill section of Bertie County. The Merry Hill still apparently was built by the same ring of bootleggers who built the Concord distillery. They had a string of these giant stills across North Carolina and eastern Tennessee. Both of the huge rigs, Concord and Merry Hill, were located very close to a road, and both were virtually automatic. The electric power for both stills had been circumvented to avoid going through the meter box and running up large and suspicious electric bills. Both raids resulted in the confiscation of several motor vehicles. The major difference between the Concord still and the Merry Hill still was the mash capacity. The Concord still had a mash capacity of thirteen thousand gallons while the Merry Hill moonshine factory's mash capacity was over

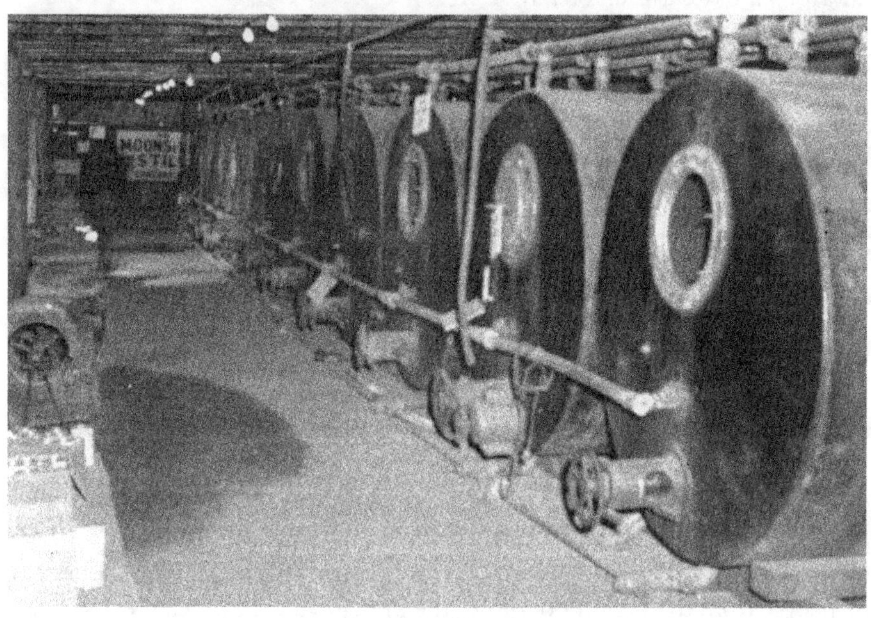

This massive underground moonshine factory near Midland in Cabarrus County was raided on March 15, 1968, by federal, state and local moonshine raiders, including ATF agent Robert Martin. The still was similar in design and operation to other large stills found in eastern Tennessee and western and eastern North Carolina. *Courtesy of Manuel Kiser and the* Concord Tribune.

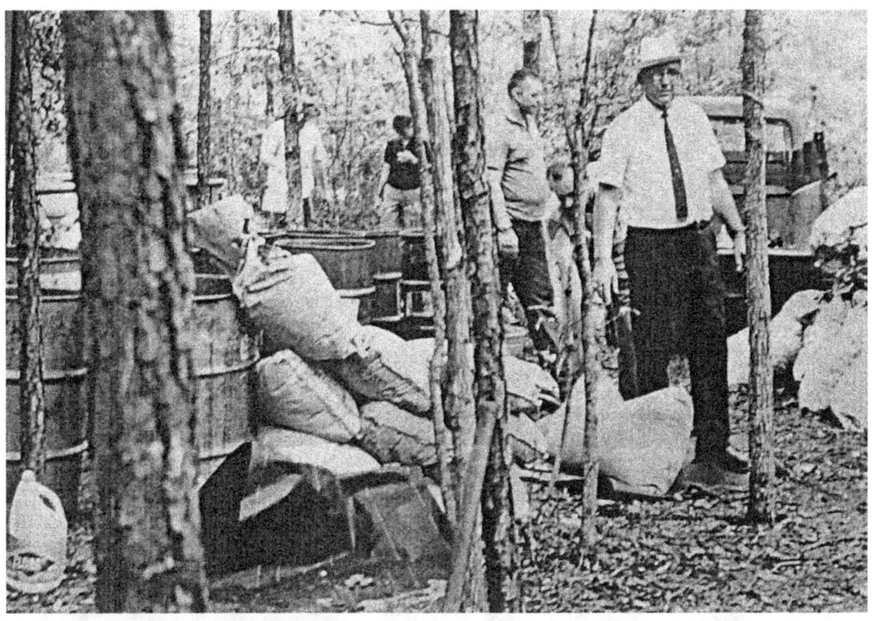

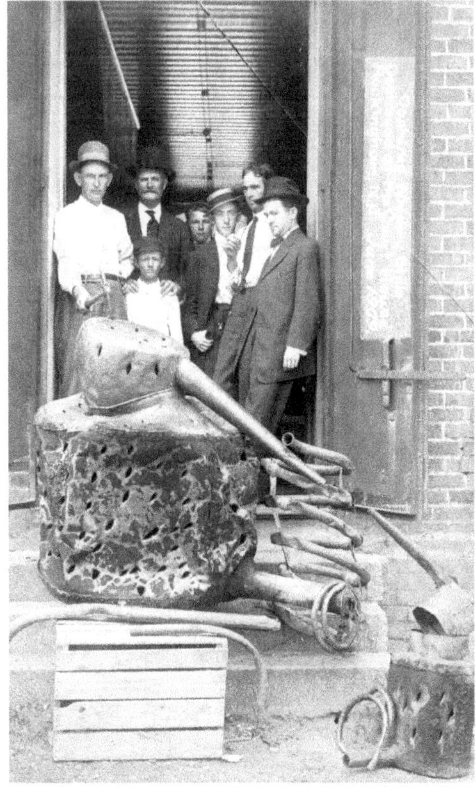

Above: This huge still, with a capacity of 13,450 gallons of mash, was captured near Bunn in Franklin County on April 1, 1969. *Courtesy of Johnny Binkley.*

Left: Captured whiskey stills, destroyed at Court House, Rockingham, North Carolina, June 1909. *Courtesy of State Archives of North Carolina.*

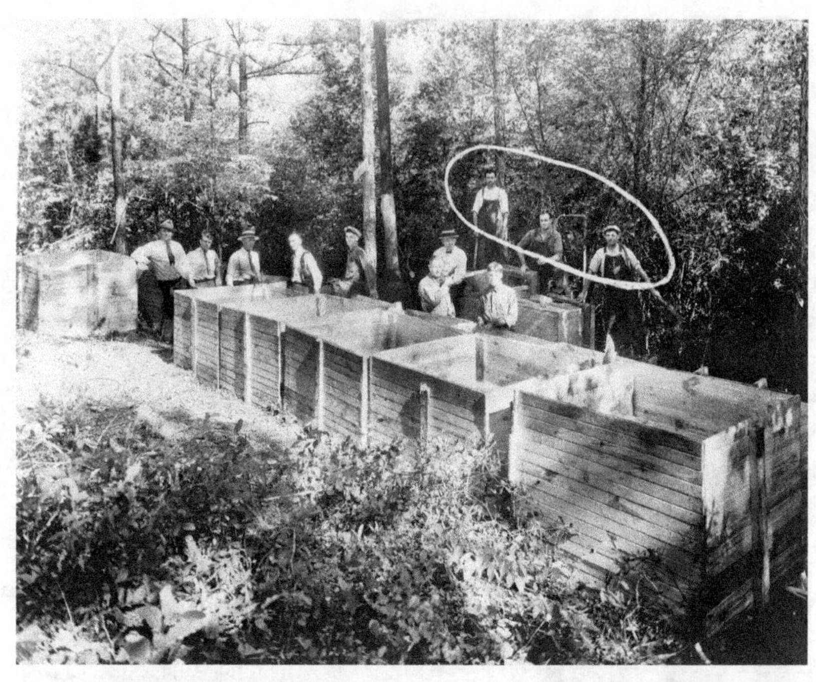

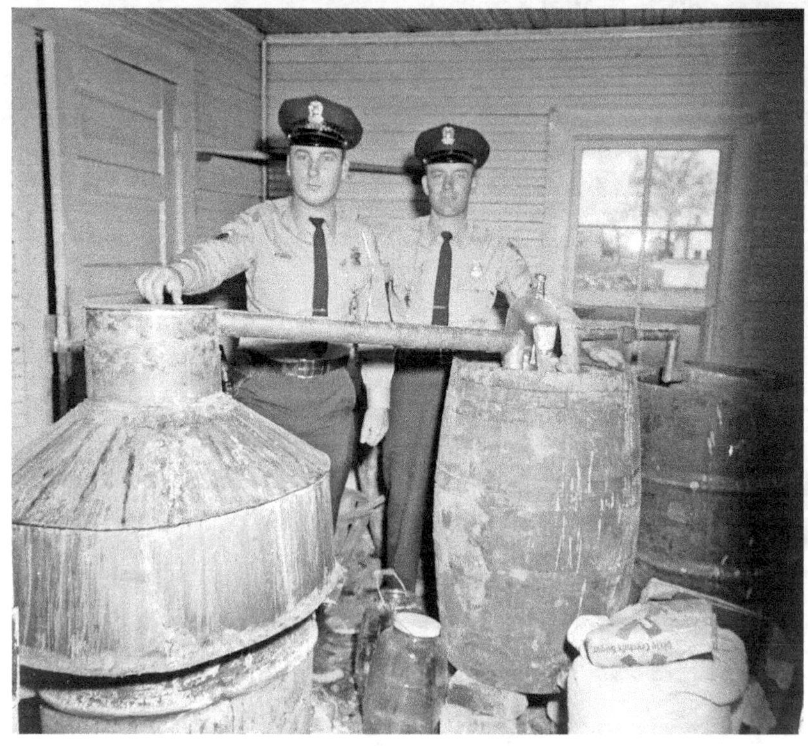

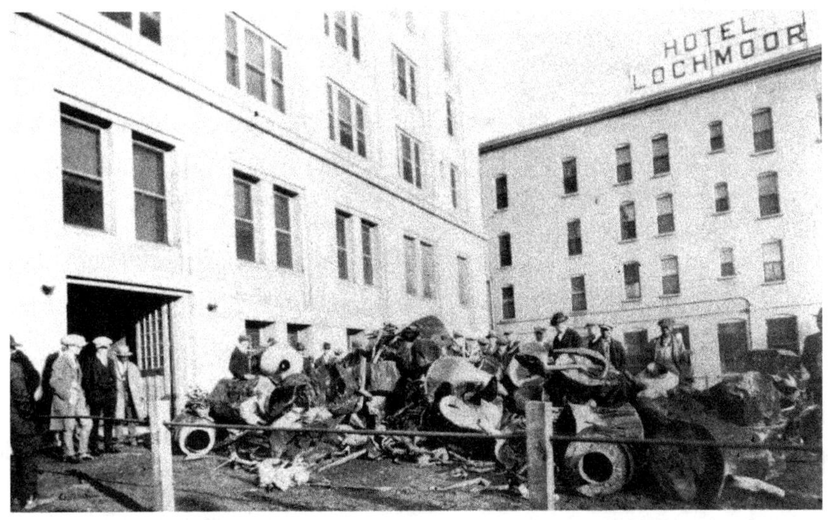

Whiskey stills, Durham, North Carolina, 1923. *Courtesy of State Archives of North Carolina.*

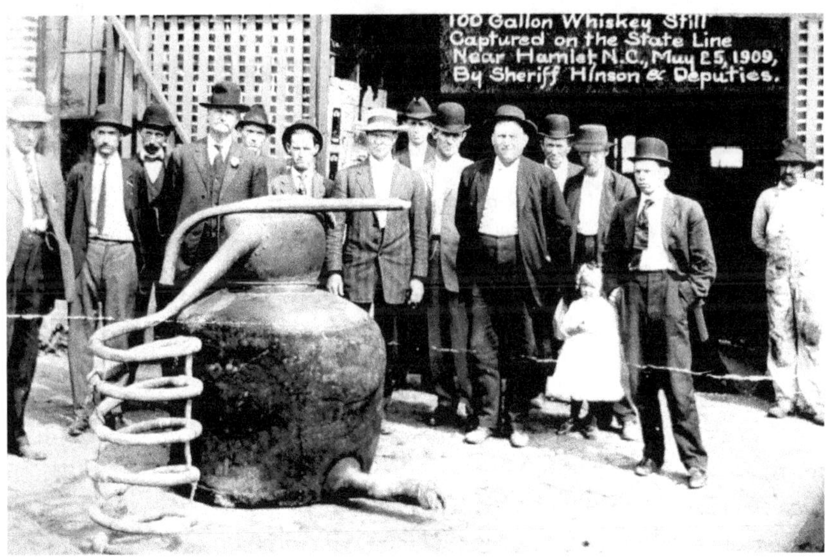

In Hamlet, a one-hundred-gallon whiskey still was captured by Sheriff Hinson and deputies on May 25, 1909. *Courtesy of State Archives of North Carolina.*

Opposite, top: Image of men at a moonshine still near High Point, circa 1927. *Courtesy of North Carolina Collection, University of North Carolina–Chapel Hill.*

Opposite, bottom: Image of two law enforcement officers standing behind an illegal still in February 1961 in Greensboro, North Carolina. *Charles S. Killebrew Collection, North Carolina Collection, University of North Carolina–Chapel* Hill.

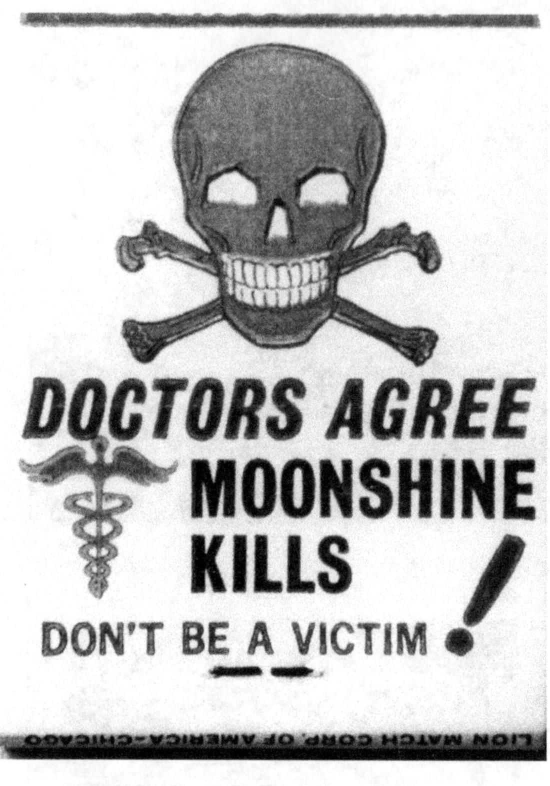

Matchbook that was utilized by ATF in its fight against North Carolina bootleggers. *Courtesy of Phillip McGuire.*

sixteen thousand. Another difference between the two giant rigs was the way they were concealed from public view. The Concord still was completely underground while the Merry Hill distillery was hidden under a house trailer and disguised as a family home with playground equipment and dog kennels visible from the road. Moonshine raiders had made several trips by both sites before they were finally able to discover the hidden stills. It was obvious to the moonshine raiders that whoever designed and built the two jumbo factory stills had an extensive knowledge of and a deep experience in the manufacture of liquor. The moonshine raiders also believed that the mastermind behind the Concord and Merry Hill stills and several others similar to them was originally from Wilkes County. Several federal moonshine raiders have indicated that they have reason to believe that the giant moonshine factory that was found at Malpass Corner near Magnolia in Pender County on October 11, 1973, can be traced back to the same bootlegger who designed the Concord and Merry Hill moonshine factories. The Merry Hill and Malpas Corner (Magnolia) stills each had a mobile home associated with them. The suspected mastermind was never arrested for his alleged connection to any of the giant stills.

Chapter 3

MOUNTAIN REGION

North Carolina's High Country Moonshine

The mountain region, the smallest of North Carolina's three geographical regions, is generally recognized as the birthplace of the state's colorful and vibrant moonshine legacy, which was created by the influx of Scotch-Irish immigrants into the region in the 1700s. These immigrants brought with them the recipes and knowledge for making whiskey, which they produced as a means for their economic survival. When conversation turns to North Carolina moonshine, the mountain region more often than not comes to mind. Many citizens of the state believe that the mountain region is the gateway to North Carolina moonshine. The region extends from Alleghany County in the northeast corner of the region to Cherokee County in the very western tip of North Carolina. Asheville in Buncombe County is the largest city in the mountain region, followed by slightly smaller cities like Boone, Morganton, Lenoir, Hendersonville and Cullowhee.

The mountain region is home to such famous entities as Grandfather Mountain, the Great Smokey Mountains, the Blue Ridge Parkway and the Lin Cove Viaduct. The region is also home to numerous institutions of higher learning, including the University of North Carolina–Asheville, Appalachian State University, Western Carolina University, Mars Hill College, Brevard University and Montreat College, each of which houses archival materials on the long and extensive moonshine legacy of the mountains of North Carolina. More books, stories and articles have been written about moonshine in the mountains than any other section of North Carolina. There is a general and growing consensus across the state that the

WARNING

Posters like this one were made by ATF to combat moonshine operations in North Carolina. *Courtesy of Phillip McGuire.*

mountain region is the "grandfather" of North Carolina moonshine. From Bear Point Creek in Cherokee County to Moss Run Branch in Wilkes County, unprecedented amounts of moonshine poured out of the mountains of North Carolina to thirsty booze guzzlers from Chicago to New Orleans and untold numbers of destinations elsewhere.

While the names of such North Carolina moonshine icons as Lewis Redmond, Marvin "Popcorn" Sutton and Junior Johnson are synonymous with the enormous fame of the region, hundreds of other mountain bootleggers practiced their whiskey-making craft practically unnoticed. A few would occasionally make news on the front page of local newspapers when they were arrested for making moonshine, but for the most part, many of those have quietly slipped into obscurity.

The mountain region is home to Wilkes County, the moonshine production mecca and Moonshine Capital of the World (according to some), a nickname first credited to Vance Packard in his article on Wilkes County moonshine titled "Millions in Moonshine" that appeared in the September 1950 issue of *The American* magazine. Some students and observers of North Carolina moonshine have described Wilkes County as the "ground zero for North Carolina moonshine." Wilkes County is also

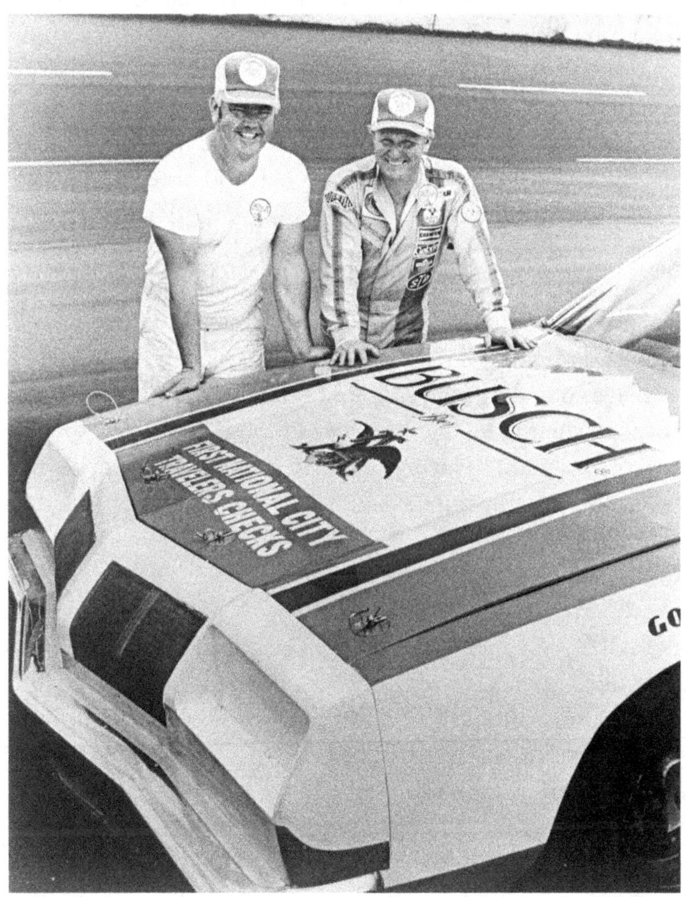

One of the great moonshine figures of North Carolina and NASCAR Hall of Famer Junior Johnson (*left*) is seen here with fellow NASCAR driver Cale Yarborough. *Courtesy of the State Archives of North Carolina.*

considered the birthplace of NASCAR, Lowe's Foods and Lowe's Home Improvement Company.

Wilkes County became Junior Johnson's personal racetrack, where he rolled as a highly skilled moonshine hauler after his father taught him how to elude the feds and long before he received his North Carolina driver's license. Johnson, following years of running moonshine, turned his attention to auto racing, where he became one of the founding and dominating drivers of NASCAR and a very popular member of its hall of fame. Johnson's fame is legendary. He became known as the "Last American Hero" in Tom Wolfe's article about him that appeared in the *New Yorker* in 1996.

Haywood County's native son Marvin "Popcorn" Sutton, who was born in Maggie Valley on October 5, 1946, became another of the state's most famous bootleggers. Sutton became the subject of numerous books and newspaper articles, as well as a documentary, which helped propel him to be called the "Paul Bunyan of Moonshine" following his death on March 16, 2009.

Curtis Nichols and his wife, Rose, brother and sister-in-law of Barbara Nichols Mulder, coauthor of this book, described with great fondness their experiences of meeting and visiting with Popcorn Sutton on their vacations to Maggie Valley. Frank Stephenson and Mulder believe that these experiences are a testament to why Popcorn Sutton was so well liked and why his fame had no boundaries. The Nichols couple from Suffolk, Virginia, chuckled when asked about the sign that hung on the front door to Popcorn Sutton's store at Maggie Valley. The sign supposedly read, "Never mind the dog, beware of the man!" During one of the Nicholses' visits with Popcorn Sutton, the famous moonshiner asked Curtis if he had ever tasted any of his stuff (meaning his moonshine).

"Don't think I have," Curtis replied.

"Follow me," Popcorn Sutton motioned to a backroom door that led to a storage room. The two men entered the room, and Sutton walked over to a cabinet and pulled open a drawer that contained pint jars full of moonshine.

"Do you see these bubbles?" Sutton pointed to some small bubbles that were floating on top of the moonshine.

"Yeah, I see them," Curtis replied.

"Do you know what those bubbles mean?" Sutton asked.

Curtis shook his head, "I don't know."

Sutton grinned. "Those bubbles tell us that it is damn good stuff. Would you like a little taste?"

"Yes I would," Curtis replied and sipped from a pint jar that Sutton handed to him. "Stuff is kind of smooth—never tasted any like that before."

"Glad you like," Sutton grinned.

"Looks like you stay pretty busy here during the summer months with all these folks coming in your place. What do you do in the winter when it is cold up here and the tourists are gone?" Curtis asked.

"Make a little...," Sutton smiled.

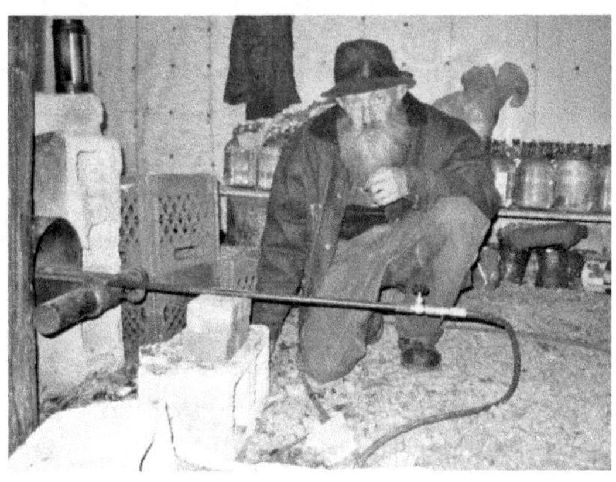

Marvin "Popcorn" Sutton, following his death in 2009, became known as the "Paul Bunyan of Moonshine." *Courtesy of Neal Hutchinson, Sucker Punch Pictures.*

"I hear you," Curtis laughed. The Nicholses were saddened when they learned that Popcorn Sutton had taken his own life on March 16, 2009, in order to avoid going back to federal prison following a moonshine-related conviction in 2008. They would have attended Popcorn Sutton's funeral service if they had known about it in time. The funeral, which was held in Dandridge, Tennessee, seven months following Popcorn Sutton's death, was attended by a large crowd, including country music star Hank Williams Jr. It is interesting to note that one of the bootleggers who were arrested in May 1972 in connection with the giant moonshine factory still at Merry Hill in Bertie County, North Carolina, was from Dandridge, Tennessee.

Since the mountain region had the distinction of probably being the largest producer of moonshine ever in the state, there was always an unusually large presence of local, state and federal moonshine raiders there, particularly in Wilkes County. These liquor police were a proud and tough breed of highly qualified, honorable and well-respected men. Their loyalty to their profession was rock solid and beyond any reproach regardless of where they worked in the state. Their work was not without risk to life and limb. Some of them chased bootleggers for only a few years. Some spent a lifetime chasing moonshiners of all descriptions all over North Carolina's high country and all of the state, for that matter. Many moonshine raiders applied their craft of chasing liquor and busting bootleggers quietly and received well-earned and much-deserved pins, plaques, framed certificates of appreciation and gold watches at their retirements. Occasionally, moonshine raiders who had fought the liquor wars and had chased bootleggers all their lives were recognized in various and sometimes special ways.

One excellent example of this is the late Charles Sylvester Felts, who was a federal ATF agent in Wilkes County for thirty years. Felts's exemplary liquor-chasing career was covered extensively in books, newspaper stories and magazines, including Vance Packard's article, "Millions in Moonshine." The extensive news coverage clearly documents why Felts acquired the title "Mr. Revenuer" of Wilkes County, where his record of confiscating over five million gallons of mash and over seventy thousand gallons of rotgut and making over 2,500 moonshine-related arrests stand today as a remarkable testament of hard work, loyalty, integrity and dedication to the craft and the profession of being a liquor policeman.

A World War I veteran, Felts was a native of Wilkes County, having been born in the community of Hays on May 20, 1891. He died on December 9, 1972, and was interred in Mountlawn Memorial Park in North Wilkesboro. The remarkable legacy of Felts prompted the North Carolina Department of Transportation in June 2015 to name a section of North Carolina Highway 18 in Wilkes County in his honor. This section of the highway is now known as the Charles S. Felts Highway. This renaming is in one respect a testament to the character and true grit of the local, state and federal men who worked all across the state as moonshine raiders. In the fall of 2016, Felts was inducted into the Wilkes County Hall of Fame.

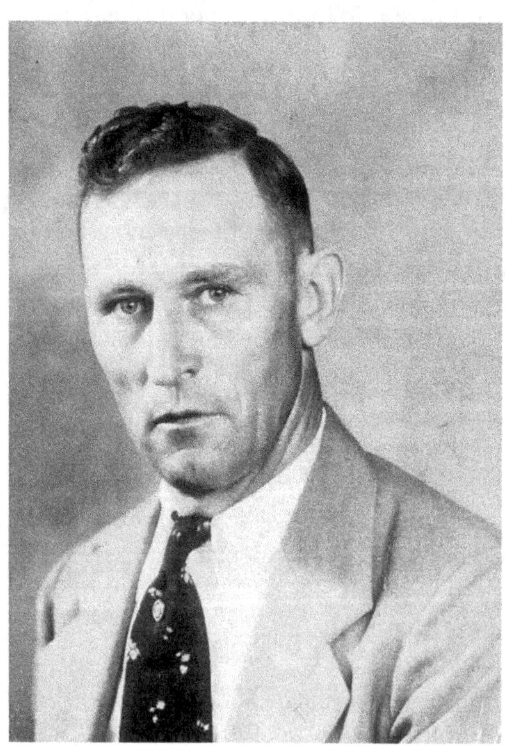

Charles Sylvester Felts. *Courtesy of the Charles S. Felts family.*

Another mountain moonshine raider, Phillip C. McGuire, a native of neighboring Watauga County, carved out a stellar career with ATF. McGuire, who was the youngest man to ever be appointed an ATF agent, rose through the ranks to become associate director of ATF in Washington, D.C. Early in his exemplary and far-reaching career, McGuire worked a number of years undercover without backup

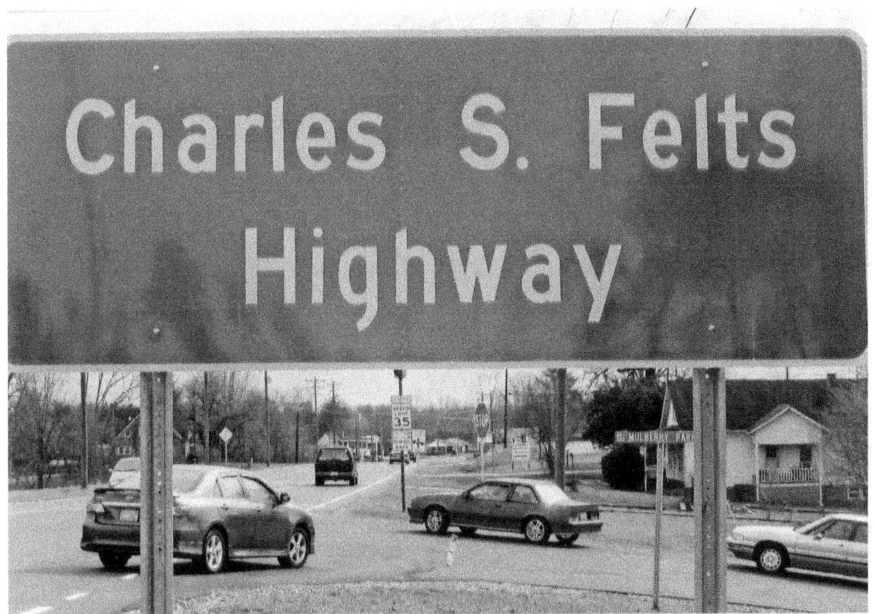

The North Carolina Department of Transportation named this five-mile section of NC Highway 18 in Wilkes County in honor of Charles Sylvester Felts, who had over 2,500 moonshine-related arrests during his long career as a law enforcement officer. *Courtesy of Phillip McGuire.*

in the moonshine business. His eldest son was born under an assumed name because of his father's undercover work, which at times placed him in extreme danger. In the mid-1960s, McGuire was working undercover in eastern North Carolina when the bootlegger whom he was trying to purchase liquor from made him disrobe because he suspected McGuire of being a federal agent. When the bootlegger could not prove his suspicion, he fired a weapon over McGuire's head, resulting in major hearing loss for the undercover ATF agent.

McGuire stated, "My main targets were not the small Snuffy Smith–type bootleggers but the organized moonshiners who operated highly sophisticated factory stills." A case in point was the big still that McGuire, along with some of his ATF colleagues and local officers, worked in 1972 in Merry Hill. The Merry Hill factory still belonged to a group of bootleggers who operated giant stills in three states: North Carolina, Tennessee and South Carolina. In 1986, President Ronald Reagan honored McGuire with the award of Meritorious Executive for his outstanding service.

So why was Wilkes County such a prolific producer of moonshine that it became known as the Moonshine Capital of the World? One reason might be

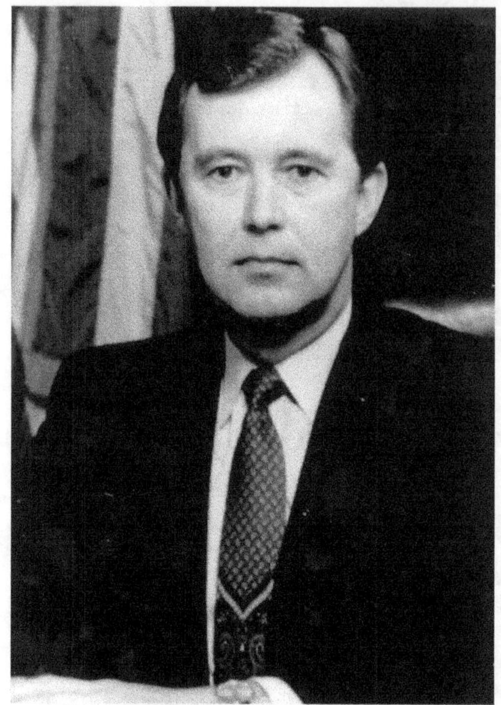

Left: Phillip McGuire was the youngest man ever to be appointed an ATF agent. He rose through the ranks to become associate director of ATF in Washington, D.C. *Courtesy of Phillip McGuire.*

Below: "Crooked Whiskey in Western North Carolina," from the August 23, 1879 edition of *Harper's Weekly*, shows a moonshiner and his still in North Carolina. *Courtesy of the State Archives of North Carolina.*

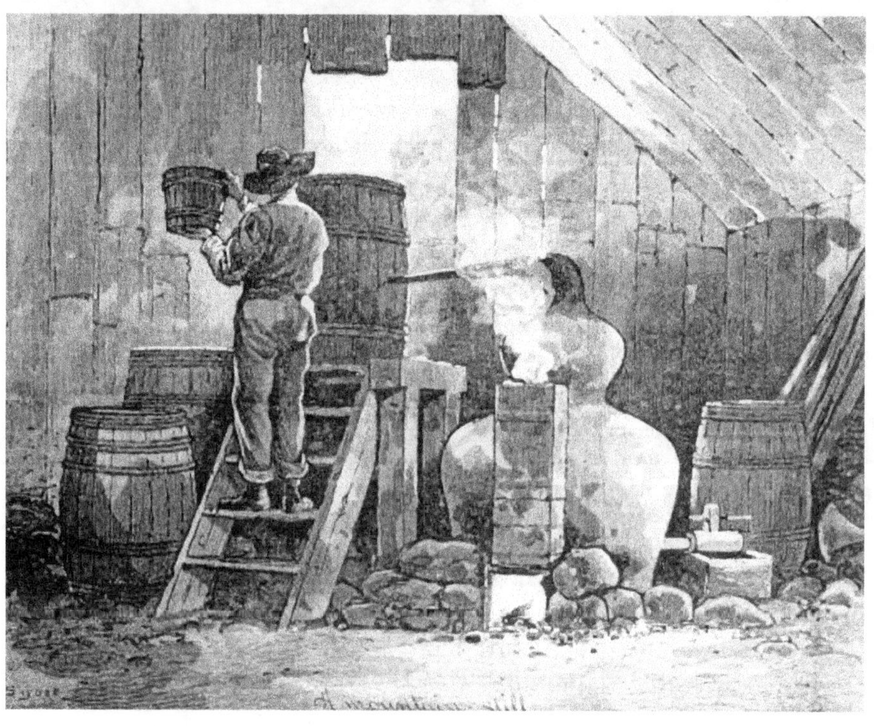

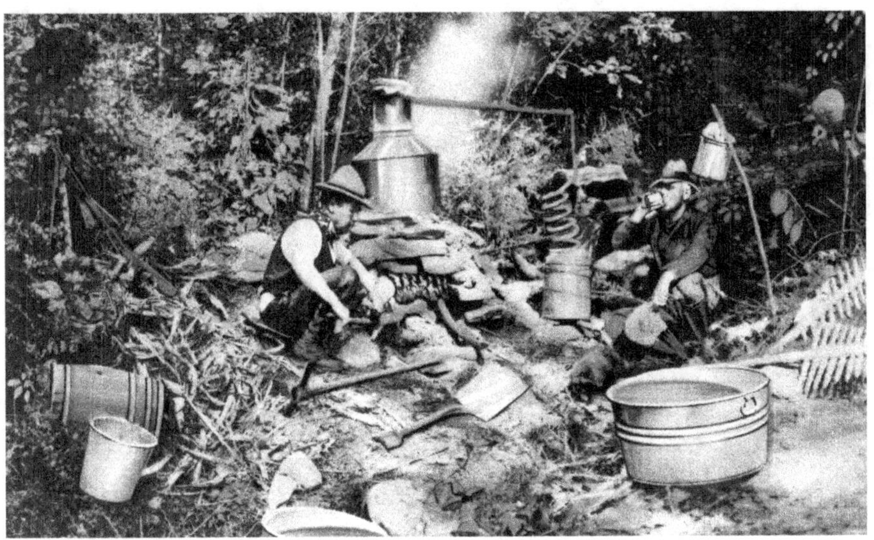

A typical moonshine still in the heart of the mountains. *Courtesy of State Archives of North Carolina.*

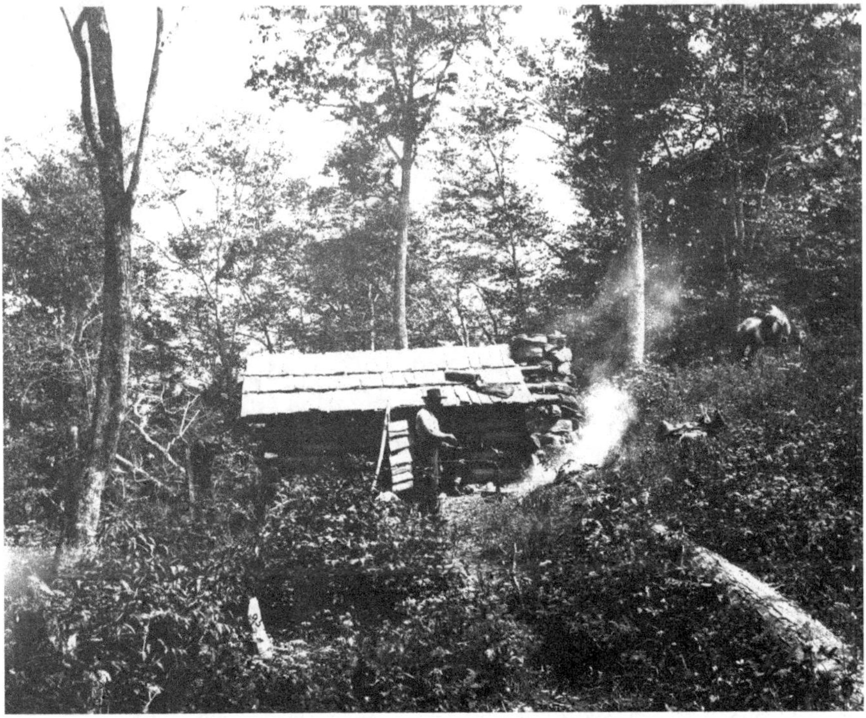

Still shelter, shakes roof and mountains, circa 1896. *Courtesy of State Archives of North Carolina.*

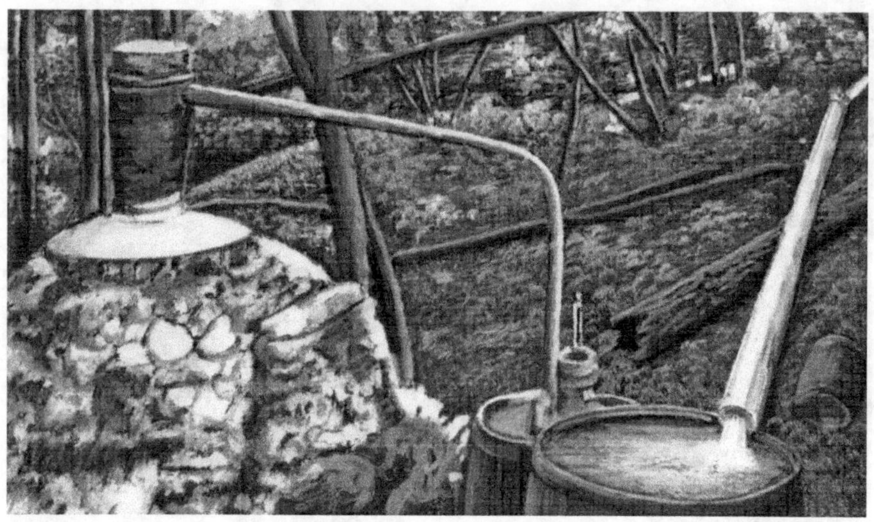

This postcard shows an eighty-gallon moonshine still in the heart of the mountains. *Courtesy of Pack Memorial Library.*

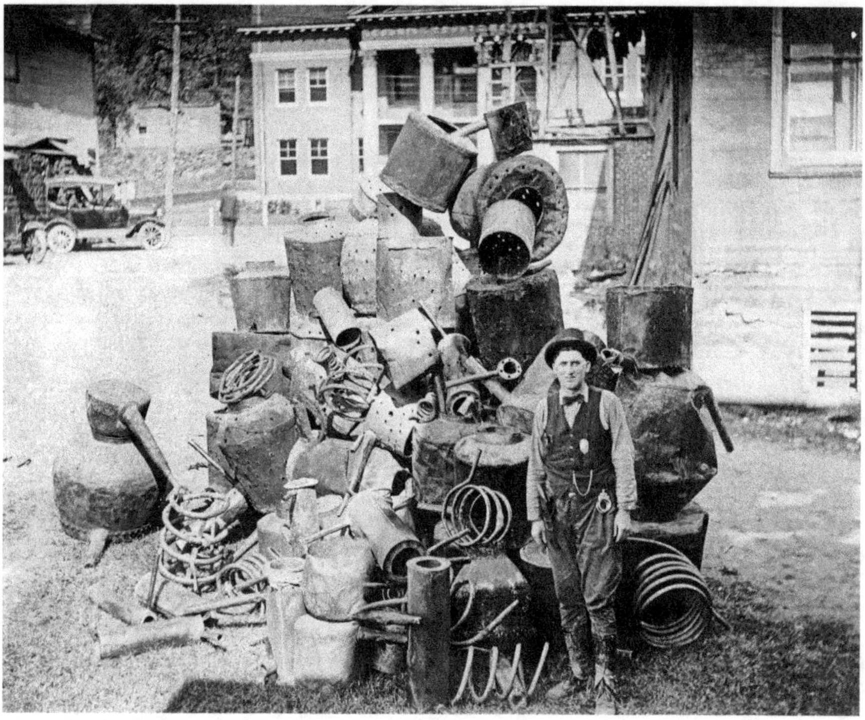

Marshal Liquor Traffic, August 1921 in the North Carolina Photographic Collection, #P0001. *Courtesy of North Carolina Collection Photographic Archives, The Wilson Library, University of North Carolina–Chapel Hill.*

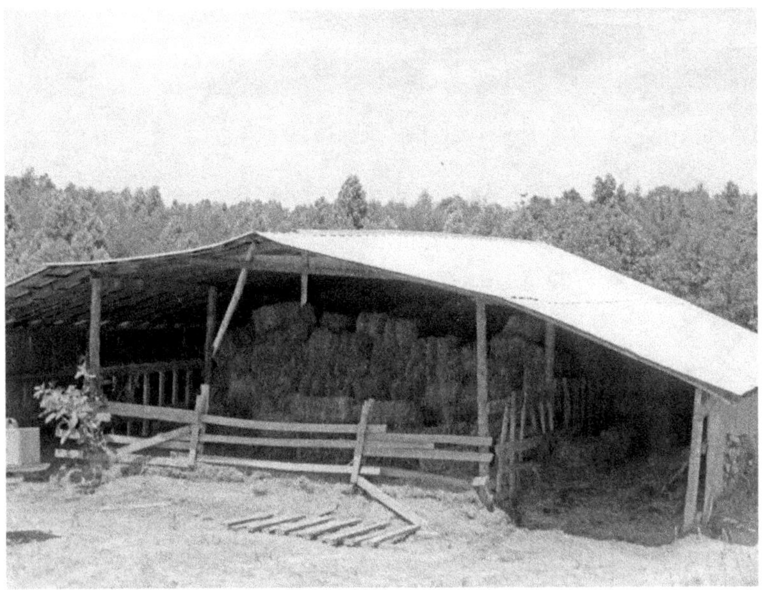

ATF agent Phillip McGuire, along with other ATF agents, found a large still underneath this barn in Wilkes County in the late 1960s. *Courtesy of Phillip McGuire.*

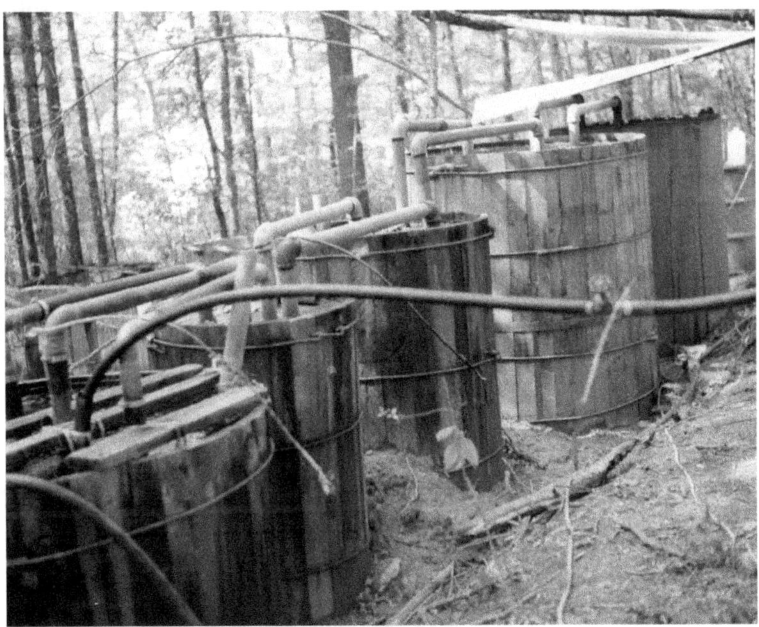

This Ashe County still was raided by ATF agent Phillip McGuire and other ATF agents in July 1971. *Courtesy of Phillip McGuire.*

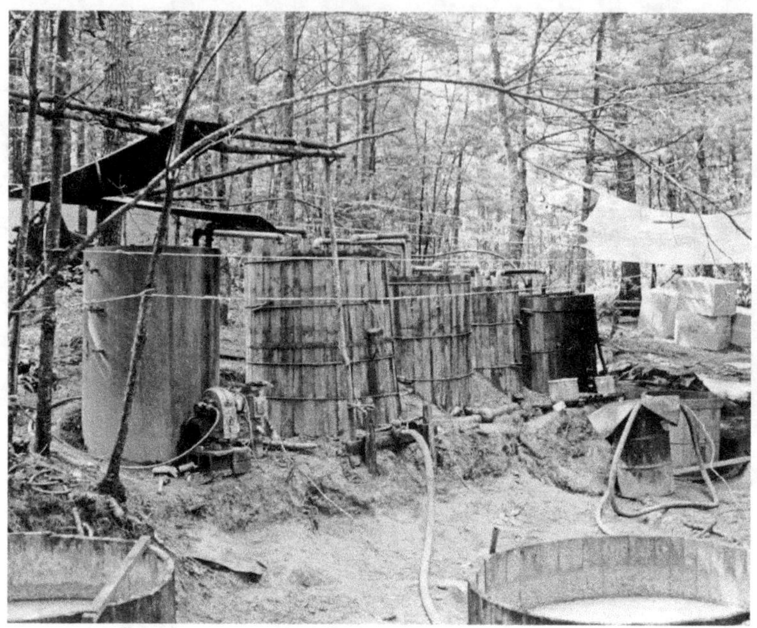

ATF moonshine raiders raided this still near West Jefferson in July 1971. *Courtesy of Phillip McGuire.*

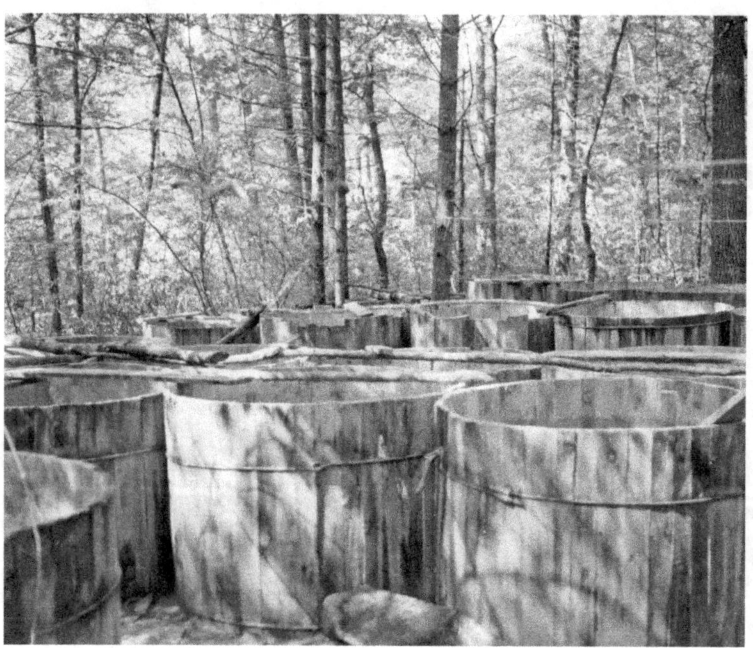

This still was taken in Ashe County in July 1971 by ATF agents. *Courtesy of Phillip McGuire.*

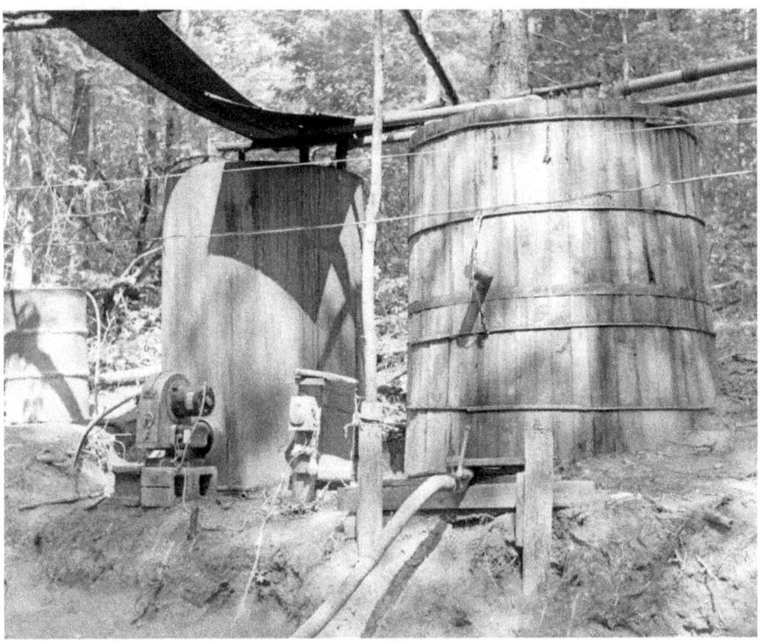

ATF agent Phillip McGuire along with other ATF agents hit this large still in July 1971 near West Jefferson. *Courtesy of Phillip McGuire.*

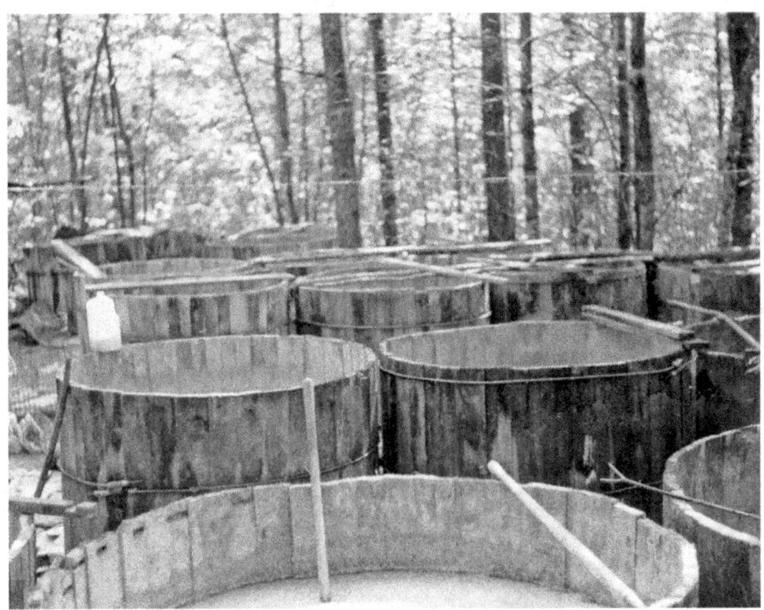

This Ashe County moonshine factory was taken by ATF agent Phillip McGuire along with other ATF agents in July 1971. *Courtesy of Phillip McGuire.*

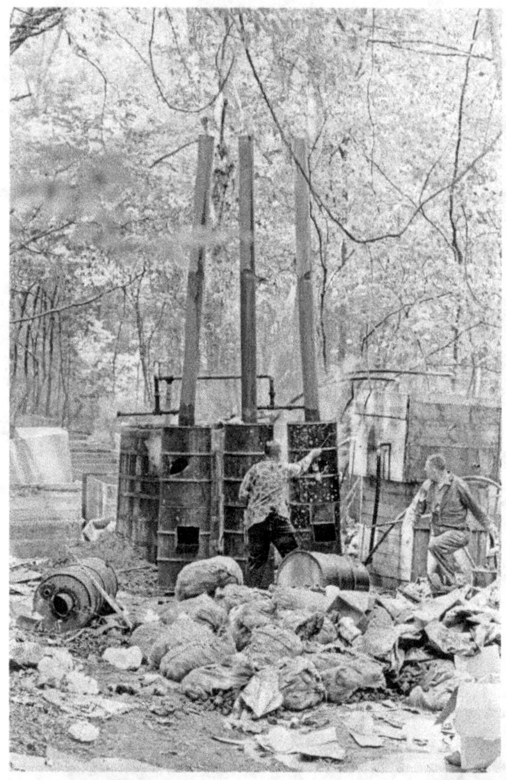

Left: In the late 1960s, Agent Phillip McGuire with other moonshine raiders found this still in Yadkin County. *Courtesy of Phillip McGuire.*

Below: Moonshine raiders *(from left to right)* Jack Whisnant, Fred Hennessee and James Williams with jars of moonshine among beehives at a raid in Burke County, circa 1970. *Courtesy of the* (Morganton) News Herald, *Morganton, North Carolina.*

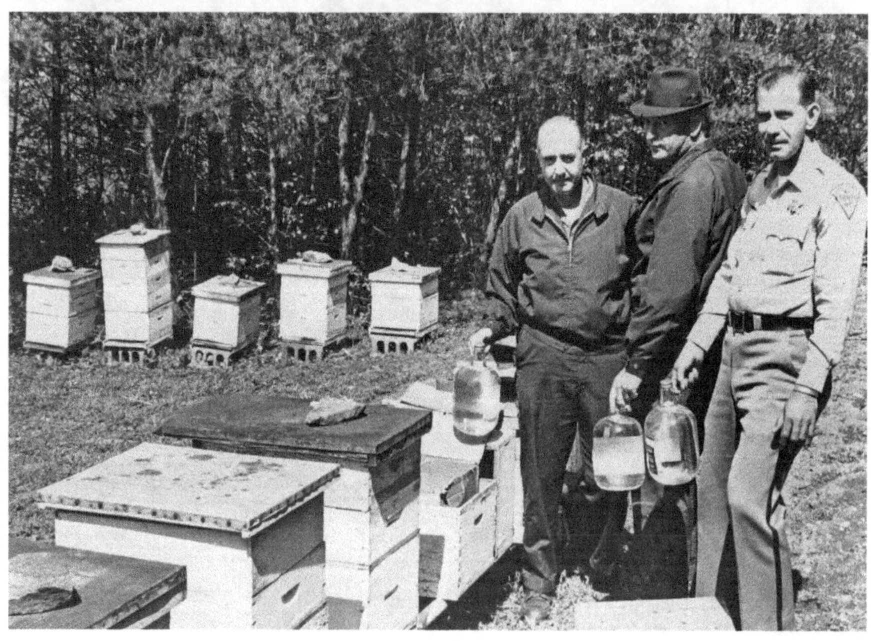

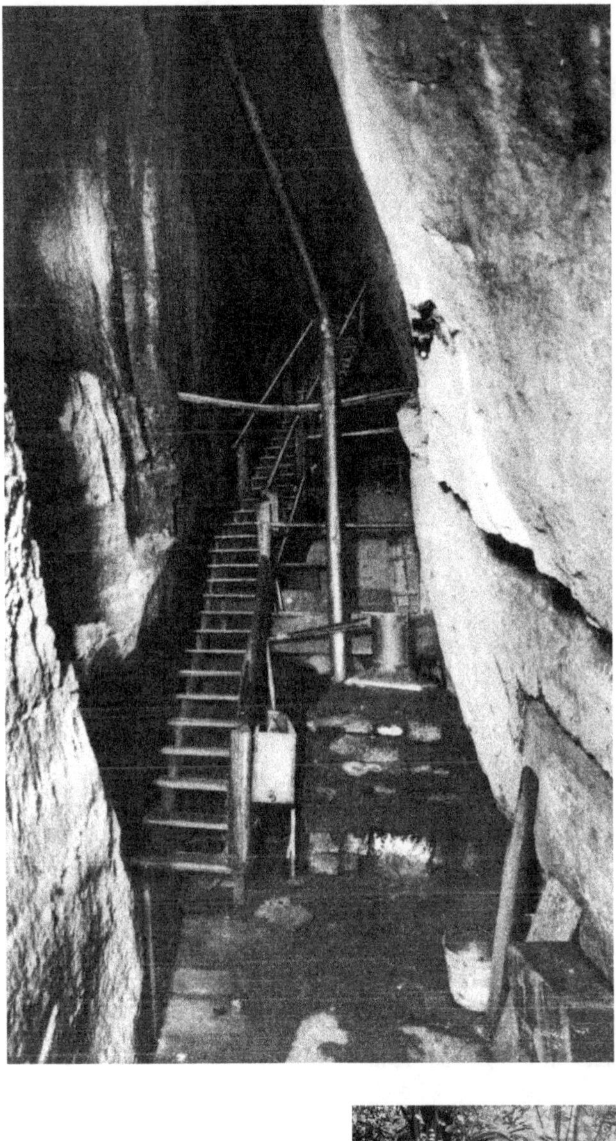

Moonshiners Cave, Chimney Rick, western North Carolina. *Courtesy of the State Archives of North Carolina.*

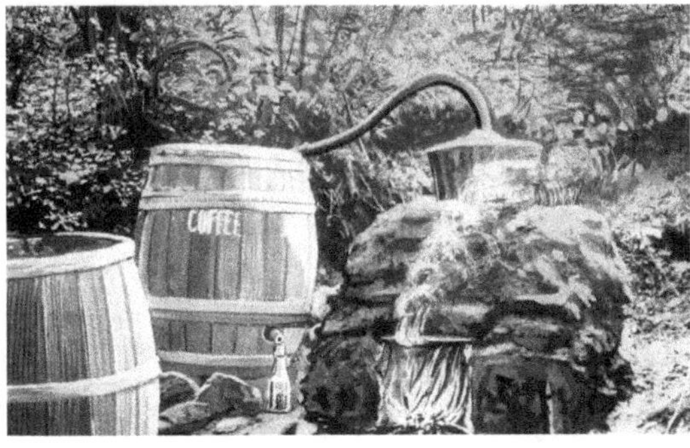

Postcard of making moonshine in the "land of the sky," or the area around Asheville. *Courtesy of Pack Memorial Library.*

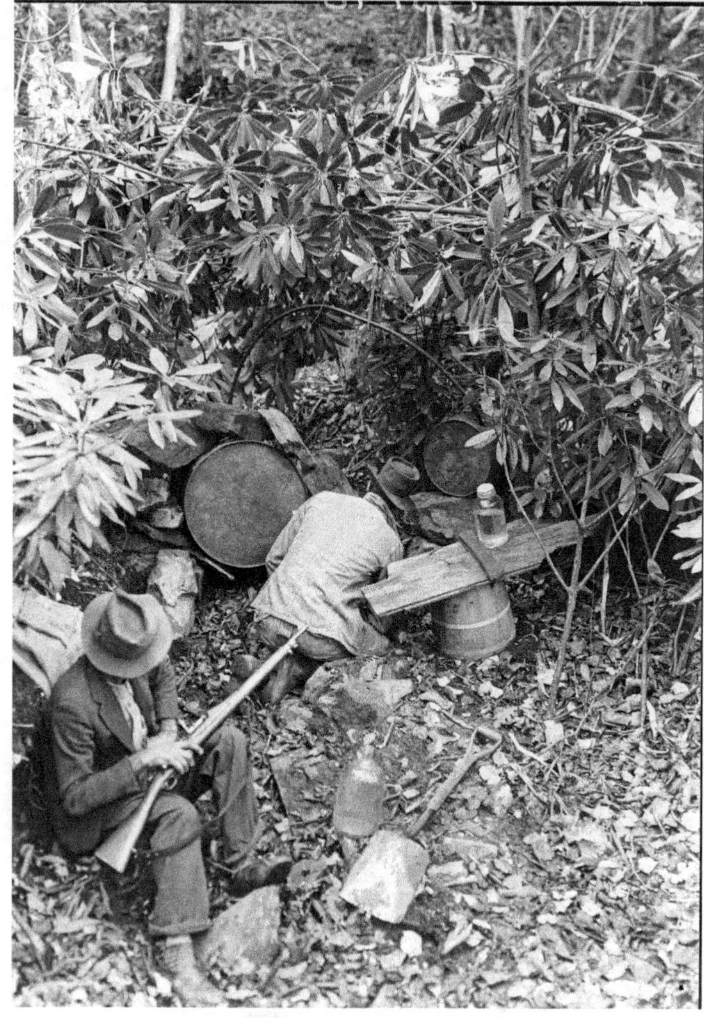

UNC Illegal Distillers, circa 1904–1954 in the Bayard Morgan Wootten Photographic Collection #P0011. *Courtesy of North Carolina Collection, University of North Carolina–Chapel Hill.*

attributed to the kind of soil that is found in Wilkes County. Apparently it is not very conductive to growing hugely profitable crops, so for years, many of the county's citizens turned to the making of moonshine for their very economic survival. At one time, tobacco was a profitable crop grown in Wilkes County, but not everyone grew tobacco. Today, with the moonshine-fostered economy all but disappeared, the poultry giant Tyson Foods is a major employer in the county, and wine and cattle production is growing.

Chapter 4

ANVIL HEAD, HONEY DRIPPER AND CYCLOPS

Strange Moonshine Raider Encounters

Most veteran moonshine raiders would agree that no two raids on North Carolina bootleg operations were the same. Hundreds of North Carolina moonshine raids were mundane and went off without any incidents or strange encounters happening. The raiders would go in, bust up the rig and leave. But there were accounts of a number of moonshine raids that were anything but the norm. The strange encounters were not limited to one geographical region of North Carolina. Frank Stephenson can remember many classic cases from childhood and when he worked with his father as a moonshine raider.

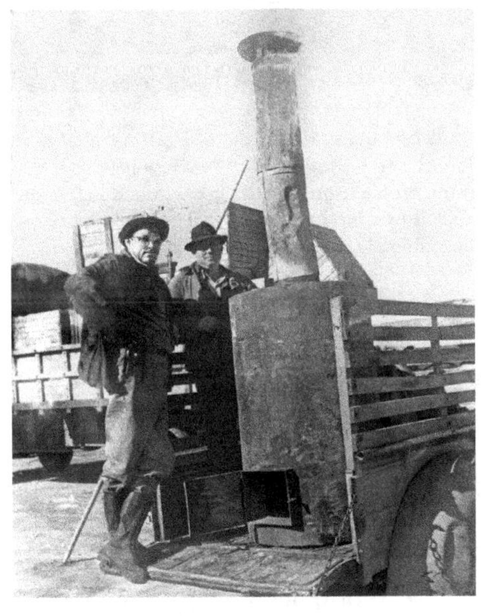

Hertford County deputy Frank Stephenson Sr. (*left*) and his brother John H. Stephenson with boiler and vats seized at large still that was raided in northern Hertford County on December 11, 1953, by Deputy Stephenson and crew, including his son, Frank Stephenson Jr. The still belonged to a group of bootleggers from Virginia. *Photograph by F. Roy Johnson.*

My very first encounter with moonshine occurred when I was

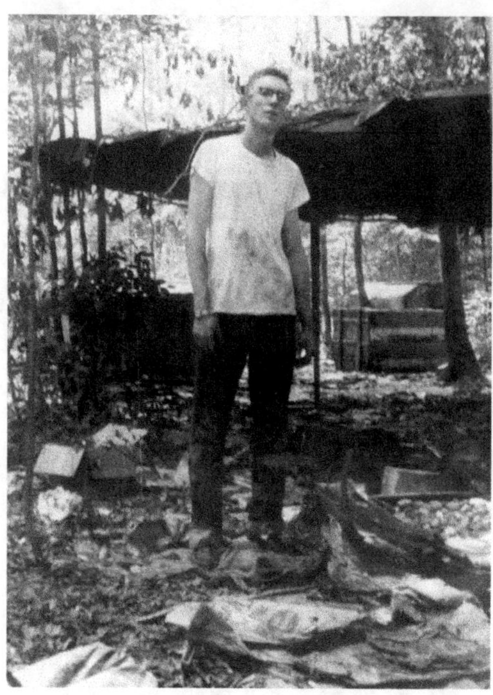

Frank Stephenson Jr. in the still yard of a large still that he and his father, Hertford County deputy Frank Stephenson Sr., and crew raided in Maney's Neck Township in northern Hertford County on December 11, 1953. *Photograph by F. Roy Johnson.*

about six years old, shortly after my late father, Frank Stephenson Sr., came home following World War II and signed on as a part-time deputy with the Hertford County Sheriff's Department in Winton. My initial introduction to moonshine happened one morning when my father and I were cane pole fishing on the Meherrin River about four miles south of Murfreesboro. We were in a juniper boat that my father had made, and we were fishing at the mouth of a small creek when suddenly yellow sugar bags came floating out of the creek into the Meherrin River right in front of us. My father told me to pull my line in, and we quietly eased our way up the creek, where we found a small still sitting on the creek bank. My father loaded the condenser, or copper coil (sometimes called a worm); some hand tools; and about two hundred pounds of sugar in our boat. Then he pushed the six oak barrels of fermenting mash over and chopped holes in them with an axe that he found in the still yard. He also broke over sixty half-gallon jars that were at the still. The sugar that my father seized at this and other stills was always given to needy families in the community if it was not bug or ant infested. My very first moonshine encounter was both fascinating and unforgettable, as were scores and scores of other moonshine raids that I accompanied my father on over the course of the next ten years. A number of the more memorable, sometimes bizarre and comical encounters that we experienced on some of these raids are described in this chapter. Similar encounters from other sections are also included.

My father could take care of himself and could become rough, prickly and downright hard to deal with in a hurry. In one way, my father was sort of like a guerrilla and a Sherman tank all rolled into a General Patton–like disposition with a little sprinkle of Rodney Dangerfield and Tony Soprano thrown in. He knew the woods like a bobcat and was a powerful 250-pound soft-walking man. He taught me the art of finding and raiding stills—surveillance, smell, concealment and surprise. He told me a number of times that in order to be successful in raiding stills, you had to walk like a shadow, run like a deer and think like a bootlegger. He strongly advised that when we were going on a raid in the woods—or anywhere for that matter—to watch what I stepped on and what I stepped in because both could cause serious harm. He taught me how to drift out of sight as quietly as smoke and emerge like a ghost from the shadows. I do not remember the exact number of moonshine raids that I went on with my father, but I think it was well over one hundred, and no two of them were the same. Some of the raids were much more memorable than others; it always depended on what you encountered going to the stills, what you found at the stills or who you found at the still. As a part-time Hertford County deputy sheriff, my father received only five dollars for each worm, or condenser, that he seized and turned in to the sheriff's office in the county seat of Winton. In many cases, the five dollars per worm was hardly worth the effort, considering some of the problems and hazards that we encountered on some of the raids.

When North Carolina moonshine raiders would begin their descent on a still, they never knew what they might encounter along the way or find at the still yard. One hazy afternoon in April 1952, during a raid that my father and I were conducting up on the Boone's Bridge Road in the northern part of Hertford County, the ground cover and underbrush were moist from an earlier light shower that enabled my father and me to easily slip up on the still yard without being detected. We could smell the familiar odor of mash being run off, and we could hear a hissing sound coming from the still. As we inched closer to the still yard, we could hear the voices of at least two people. My father suddenly stopped and motioned toward the still yard, where we could clearly see a naked man and woman exchanging something a little heavier than hello and goodbye while the still was running. My father quietly eased his .38-caliber pistol out of the holster and fired off a shot in the air, which caused the wheels to run slam off everything that was going on in front of us. The man, Anvil Head, froze in his tracks while the woman quickly grabbed a couple of empty sugar bags, covered her front and crouched down behind a barrel of mash.

"Anvil Head, put some clothes on and take your woman there and get outta here before I lock you both up," my father grinned.

"Yes, suh, we sure will do that right now," Anvil Head grinned as he picked up their clothes and ran out with his naked lady following him trying to put some of her clothes back on.

Later that same year, my father had picked up creditable information that a still might be located behind a church on Possum Branch Road. On a Friday afternoon in September 1952, my father and I drove past the small country church, which was showing signs of neglect but remained active as a house of worship. My father eased his pickup truck down an old logging path and stopped. We quietly slipped out of the truck and softly walked about a thousand yards on the path, stopping when we caught the sweet smell of moonshine drifting through the air. We knew for certain that there was a still running and that it was not very far away. As we moved closer to the still, we could hear it running and clearly see a man, a woman and two young girls in the still yard. My father whispered under his breath, "Damn, look at that!" The couple at the still was Preacher Ronald "Big Head" Alphin, minister of the church, along with his wife, Erma Jane, and their two daughters, Ivey Jean and Lola Mae. The preacher was humming "What a Friend We Have in Jesus" when we quickly ran into the still yard. The four of them were totally shocked to see us there. The two girls and the wife screamed and dashed over and stood behind the minister, who appeared speechless.

"What in the world are you doing here preacher? You ain't gonna find any souls out here to save!" my father snarled.

The preacher stuttered, "Mr. Frank, you scared me to death! My house of the Lord needs a little help with paint peeling off, plaster falling down and the roof leaking mighty badly."

"Well you are going to have to find another way to help your house of the Lord because if I catch you here again, I am going to lock your mess up. Do you understand me?" my father angrily replied.

"Yes, sir, Mr. Frank. I sure do understand, and you won't ever catch me here again," the preacher replied.

"Preacher, you should be ashamed of yourself for having your wife and daughters out here in this mess," my father stated.

Later that same month, we were quietly walking a well-worn still path just off Horse Pasture Creek Road. The weather was overcast and slightly damp. We made our way up the still path to a point where we caught a whiff of the sweet smell of moonshine being run off. We peered through the underbrush toward the still, where we could see that there appeared to be only one still hand working the rig. My father motioned for me to stay put while he nimbly worked his way to the still yard, where he reached out and tapped the unsuspecting bootlegger, Hog Bear, on his right shoulder as he sat on a mash barrel eating a can of Vienna sausage. The shocked and astonished bootlegger was so surprised that he accidently messed himself up. "You, you scared me so bad that I just crapped in my pants," Hog Bear yelled.

My father laughed, "Hog Bear, go sit your ass in that barrel of mash—that'll clean you up and add flavor to rot gut at the same time."

"Naw, naw, suh, I'll go and sit in that creek over there but not in the mash barrel as that might take the skin off my mess," Hog Bear motioned.

"Sure wouldn't want anything to happen to mess up your manhood," my father laughed.

Several weeks later, my father and I were trying to locate a still at the back of the Jones farm on Hill's Ferry Road. My father eased his pickup truck along a long, winding path and finally stopped at what appeared to be the entrance to a narrow footpath. As soon as we exited the truck, we were hit with this awful smell—as if something had died nearby and was decaying. We could not immediately see anything, but it was really stinking up the area.

"Damn that sure does stink. What in the hell smells like that?" my father wondered. As soon as we began walking along the still path, we saw where the terrible odor was coming from. The odor was coming from a large dead mule that apparently had been dragged there and left without being buried. As we approached it, two large, greasy opossums ran out from a big hole in the mule's side and disappeared into the bushes. When the two opossums ran through the underbrush, we became a little concerned that the noise might have spooked any still hands who might have been at the still.

"I don't know why they didn't call Norfolk Tallow Company to come get the dead mule. They would have made soap out of it," my father noted. We continued our silent walk along the still path until we got a whiff of fermenting mash. We found a small still about two hundred yards down the path, and to our surprise, the still appeared to have been wrecked and all torn up, and the eight barrels of fermenting mash had been overturned, covering the still yard in a thick layer. But it was not hard to figure out what had happened there—we found a number of large bear tracks in the mash. "Damn. Just look at that—the bears got in the mash and tore up the still! Bears just love that mash," my father roared.

A week later, I went with my father to the Hertford County courthouse in Winton. He was supposed to testify in the case of a bootlegger he had arrested about six months earlier on Maney's Ferry Road, where General Lafayette crossed the Chowan River during his 1824–25 visit to the United

States. My father probably would not have arrested the bootlegger if he had not thrown a half-dead cottonmouth at us when we surprised him at the still. We had just taken our seats in the courtroom when Judge Anderson called for the bootlegger to go up and stand in front of him. When the bootlegger, a huge, unshaven, mean-looking white man about forty-five years old who went by the nickname Big Ugly, first stood in front of the judge, he immediately began to cry and ball his eyes out.

"Mr. Thomas, what in the world is wrong with your client there? Why is he boohooing like that in my courtroom?" the judge asked the bootlegger's lawyer.

"I don't know, your honor, never seen him all broken up like that," the lawyer replied.

The judge retorted, "Well, please tell your honey-dripper client there to stop boohooing. He's getting my courtroom floor all wet!"

"I sure will, your honor," the lawyer grinned.

One very harrowing incident happened late one afternoon a few weeks later, in June 1952, when we were crawling on the ground approaching a medium-size rig on the Big Mary Road. We were not far from the still when, all of a sudden, a large cottonmouth fell from an overhanging limb and landed right between us. Both of us immediately froze in place; we were afraid that the snake would strike if we made any movement. We also knew we had a very serious situation on our hands and that we had to be very careful whatever we did. My father blinked three times, which was our signal to roll in the opposite direction. We did manage to get out of harm's way, but in the process, we spooked the lone still hand.

As tough as the snake incident was, on the opposite side of the scale was a more humorous raid that took place behind the Henderson Farm two weeks later on a Friday afternoon. As we approached the still, my father and I nearly laughed aloud when we saw this short, fat bootlegger named Six Fingers who was constantly talking to himself. The bootlegger was called Six Fingers because he was born with six fingers on each hand. When we surprised Six Fingers, he passed out between two barrels of mash. My father woke him up by pouring a quart jar full of moonshine on his face.

One cool afternoon in February 1953 found my father and I on a raid on Gatling Road. We had walked some distance behind the old Jordan Gatling house—where Richard Jordan Gatling, inventor of the famed Gatling gun, had grown up—when we encountered the familiar smell of frying pork. Whatever was being cooked sure did smell mighty good. It reminded us of when we found a bootlegger cooking bacon and eggs at his rig. When we surprised the bootlegger, we found that while the still was running, he was cooking chitlins and fried potatoes on an old cookstove that he had apparently hauled to the still. The bootlegger, who went by the nickname of Cyclops, was singing "The Old Rugged Cross" while cooking. The bootlegger's face had been badly disfigured in a log woods accident. He had lost one eye completely, and the other eye grossly bulged out in the center of his face. Since my father and I both liked chitlins, we turned over two of the fifty-five-gallon mash barrels, sat on them and ate the cooked chitlins and fries right there because they were too good to toss out. My father admonished the bootlegger, telling him, "Cyclops, go home and don't let me ever catch you back here again." After we had eaten the chitlins, my father stood up, did several little dance like moves and said, "They were so good that it makes me wanna do the chitlin two step!"

A year later on a raid on the Mount Zion road, we found some more food cooking on an improvised stove. The bootlegger, who apparently was spooked and took off, had been cooking a mess of corned herring fish that smelled mighty good. My father and I ate four or five of the corned herring before we broke up the still. A few days later, during a late afternoon raid off Big Mary Road, we surprised a pudgy bootlegger who was popping popcorn on top of the cooker. We sampled the popcorn, which did not taste half bad. Once in a while, we found other foodstuffs cooking at stills, but since we could not tell what it was, we left it alone.

In mid-August 1953, my father and I were searching for a still up on Bull Hill Road. It was hot and steamy, and the bugs and yellow flies were particularly bad. After a brief time, we were able to locate what appeared to be the still path and quietly began walking it. After we had walked about thirty yards up the path, two wild turkeys scurried off into the thick brush to the right. We had walked about another twenty-five yards farther up the path when my father let out this horrible yell. He had accidently stepped too close to a large snapping turtle that was partially shielded from view by underbrush. The large snapping turtle appeared to weigh about fifteen or twenty pounds and had locked down on my father's right foot. My father hugged a nearby red oak tree and was trying to shake the snapper off his foot.

"Aaaugh, shit, get that damn thing off my foot! I don't give a crap how you do it, just get that damn thing off! Feels like he's about to bite all my damn toes off! Take my pistol and shoot the thing if you have to!"

"Hold your leg up in the air," I replied as I grabbed the snapping turtle by its tail and tried to separate him from my father's foot. The turtle did not budge.

"Do something! Shoot the damn thing! But don't shoot my foot!" my father bellowed as he continued to try to shake the turtle off his foot.

"I'm trying, I'm trying," I replied as I grabbed my father's boot and started to pull as hard as I could. The boot with the snapping turtle still locked on came off and fell in the still path.

"Thank God, that damn thing is off my foot," my father snarled as the snapping turtle crawled off with my father's boot firmly gripped in its mouth.

"Let me look at your foot. Did he break the skin?" I motioned to my father, who had pulled his sock off and was rubbing his toes.

"I don't think so, but my toes feel like a bulldozer has flat ass run over them, and they are throbbing like shit!" my father roared.

"Why don't we just go back home and forget the still," I asked.

"Hell no, we ain't going back to the house. We are going to finish what we came for and find that damn still," my father growled.

I looked again at my father's foot, which was beginning to turn purple from bruising. "You can't go on with your foot hurting like that."

"The hell I can't go on!" my father roared as he began walking up the still path with one boot on and one boot off. I knew that my father was not going to turn back. Once he had made up his mind, nothing could make him change it, including hell freezing over.

We continued silently walking up the still path and began to pick up the sweet smell of fermenting mash. The still was unattended when we entered the still yard, where we found about fifteen barrels of fermenting mash. My father stuck his bruised right foot in one of the barrels of mash and sighed, "That sure does feels mighty damn good!" We broke up the still and went home.

In late September 1953, we were on a raid off Camp Fire Tower Road, following up on a tip that my father had received. The weather was kind of strange that day. The area was covered in a shroud of low-hanging fog that hampered our visibility. As we moved softly up the still path, we could hear a heavy knocking noise that sounded like a car with a bad misfire in the engine. Since we had heard that noise on a few previous raids, we knew exactly what it was. Someone who did not know how to had fired the still to a point that it was too hot and had started knocking. If the still master was not very careful, this could cause a still to blow up, hurting anyone around it. We quickly eased into the still yard, completely surprising the lone bootlegger attending to the still. My father immediately recognized the man; he was one of the local undertakers and went by the nickname Bo Weevil.

"What are you doing out here, Bo Weevil? You're in the wrong profession. Ain't no dead folks out here for you to pick up!"

"Business has been a little slow lately. People just seem to be living longer these days," Bo Weevil replied.

"You need to stick with the business that you know of, putting dead folks in the ground, instead of making something that will make folks dumb, stupid and could possible kill them. Just get outta here and stay the hell away. Do you read me loud and clear?" my father explained in a stern voice.

"That I'll do, won't ever come out here no more," Bo Weevil replied as he walked hurriedly down the still path and disappeared. My father and I never caught him at a still again.

In mid-October1953, on a late Friday afternoon, my father turned off Old Cheshire Ferry Road and pulled the pickup truck to a stop near an abandoned farmhouse. We knew there was a still in the woods behind the house and barn because we had caught a whiff of the sweet smell of moonshine floating across the road on one of our Thursday night drives on the backroads. We very gently eased the truck doors shut and searched for the entrance to a still path. It did not take long to find the still path. We had walked about five hundred yards up the still path when we were suddenly met with gunfire in the form of a shotgun blast in the pine trees above our heads. The shotgun blast rained pine bark, pine needles and pine cones down on us. We immediately froze in our tracks, and my father whipped out his .38 revolver and fired three times in the direction of where the shotgun blast had originated. In the distance, we could hear people yelling and running through the woods. We moved very carefully and quietly along the still path until we found the rig with its eight barrels of mash. The bootleggers who had fired at us were apparently about to make a run when we surprised them because the still had been fired up and the mash was ready. My father destroyed the still, and we got soaking wet when it began pouring down rain as we cautiously walked back to the truck.

Early November 1953 found my father and I on a raid on the old Ramsey Farm Road very near the site of a German prisoner of war camp from World War II. The German POWs incarcerated here worked the cotton and peanut fields and log woods in the area while the local men were off to war. The morning air was cool, and it started to rain about the time we began walking up an old, heavily rutted logging path. The woods were already full of water from two days of earlier rains. We walked up the old logging path about four hundred yards until we found a small footpath going off to the left. My father motioned for me to follow him onto the footpath. We walked a short distance, stopping in our tracks when we began hearing some strange noises coming toward us. The noises sounded like hogs grunting or oinking. Then we saw just ahead of us two or three hogs wobbling toward us on the still path. There appeared to be something wrong with the hogs—they were staggering as if they were drunk. I asked my father, "What's wrong the hogs? They got the hog cholera?"

"Hell naw, they don't have cholera! They're drunk. Must have got in some mash somewhere. Hogs love mash about as much as bears do," my father explained.

"Who would have ever thought that?" I motioned as the hogs scattered into the bushes when we began walking again on the still path. We knew we were nearing a still because we began to smell the familiar scent of fermenting mash. We found the still with several overturned mash barrels and some more drunk hogs lying around the still yard.

"Yep, just look at that, they rooted over some of the mash barrels and got drunk," my father said.

"Will it hurt 'em?" I asked.

"I doubt it," my father laughed. "Hogs will eat just about anything. Back when I was growing up, we used to feed them household scraps from the kitchen, and that did not hurt them. They called it slopping the hogs. Shoot, I have even seen hogs eat poisonous snakes alive."

I laughed, "Bet that was something to see!" Before we broke up the still, we turned an oak mash barrel upside down, and my father and I played two games of checkers using a homemade checkerboard and checkers that we found under a small tarp covering about one hundred pounds of sugar. My father won both games—I rarely could beat him in checkers. When we left the still yard, we took fifty pounds of the sugar; the rest had holes in them, and ants had gotten in them.

In early January 1954, on a windy and snowy afternoon, we pulled off to the side of Battle's Beach Road and parked. We eased out of the pickup truck and slowly made our way up an old cart path, where we saw two sets of footprints in the light dusting of snow. My father had been told by an informant that a still was in the woods behind the old Battle house, which was no longer in use. The wind was blowing from behind our backs, which made it difficult to pick up the scent of moonshine. We had walked about a half mile when the footprints took off on a side path to the right, and about the same time, we picked up the first faint scent of fermenting mash. Shortly after we had started to walk on the side path, someone started shooting at us with what sounded like a .22 rifle. I immediately fell to the ground, and my father jumped behind a large pine tree and started firing back with his .38 pistol. He quickly unloaded his weapon, reloaded and fired several more times. Then the shots coming from in front of us suddenly stopped. We could hear what sounded like running in the opposite direction from us. My father cautiously motioned to start walking again, and we had walked about two hundred yards when we found a small filthy still that had been fired up.

"Damn, just look at that. It sure is one nasty-looking thing. Anybody drink any rotgut from that will surely have some serious intestinal problems!" he said. We destroyed the still and very carefully walked back to the truck.

Later in January the same year, we were working a still off the Cedar Chapel Road. The weather was raw and cold, and the clouds looked as if snow was going to start falling any minute. The still path was muddy and sticky, and we had to wade across several small shallow streams on the way to the still. We picked up the strong smell of fermenting mash as we walked on. Suddenly, we began to hear strange moans and groans coming from in front of us. We quickly bolted into the still yard, where we found two drunk and seriously injured bootleggers lying semiconscious on the ground. One of the bootleggers had a huge goiter on his neck, and both were bleeding from what appeared to be serious knife wounds. "Damn, they must have got drunk and cut each other. You take some of that burlap over there and stuff it in the wounds of that one, and I'll see what I can do with this one. Shake 'em. Maybe they'll wake up," my father directed.

"Wonder what caused them to cut up each other like that?" I asked my father.

"They probably got to drinking and squabbling over which one owned the still and one thing led to another," my father replied. We quickly chopped holes in the metal mash barrels and the cooker. Then we made a makeshift stretcher out of burlap bags and poles and totted the two drunk and injured bootleggers one by one out of the woods to the back of the pickup truck. After we had placed the two in the bed of the pickup we drove them to town, where Dr. Cooke sewed them up, and later they were locked up.

A few nights later, we had done an all-nighter on a still just off Whitley Road in hopes of catching the bootleggers when they came to the still. The sun had just risen when this older bootlegger came walking in with a six-pack of beer in his hand. When he reached the still yard, he popped opened one of the beers and guzzled it down and did a second one the same way. That was the first time that I had ever seen anyone have beer for breakfast. We were about to move on him when all of a sudden he reached down and snatched up a copperhead by the tail and, with a whipping-like motion, popped its head off. The copperhead's head flew off in the bushes, and the bootlegger tossed the headless poisonous snake in a nearby stream and watched it float away. That was the first time that I had ever seen someone pop a snake's head off like that. My father arrested the bootlegger, and we destroyed his still.

We started the month of February 1954 with a raid on the old Wilson farm that bordered the North Carolina–Virginia state line just below Southampton County, Virginia. My father had some creditable information that there was a still located just inside the North Carolina line, but the main access to it was by a path coming in from Virginia. He told me that this was just another of numerous "Virginia Creeper" cases, where bootleggers from Virginia would creep across the line into North Carolina to set up their rigs because it got too hot for them in Virginia. My father had previously encountered some bootleggers from Virginia, some of whom seemed to have a nastier disposition than some of the other bootleggers he had crossed paths with. My father knew the still was there, so we quietly moved to the site and sat on it. The still was located about fifteen feet inside North Carolina where the state line was well marked. After about an hour and a half, a lone bootlegger crossed over the Virginia line into North Carolina and walked into the still yard. When my father stood up, the shocked bootlegger quickly jumped back across the Virginia line and started cursing at us, "You can't touch me, you can't touch me as I am in Virginia now and you ain't got power over here! That badge you got on ain't worth a damn over here in Virginia so you and your boy there just go hell! You come over here I'll kick your ass and his, too!" The bootlegger quickly disappeared into the Virginia woods as my father yelled at him, "I'll get your ass, you just wait and see!" I knew from that familiar nasty look on my father's face that he meant every word he had yelled at the bootlegger. My father decided not to tear up the still, but he did take the copper coil as we quietly walked out. The fact that we did not destroy the rig led me to believe that my father had already figured out a way to catch the Virginia bootlegger.

Two weeks later, we headed back to the still where the Virginia bootlegger had cursed my father and me up one side and down another. My father had worked out a plan with Sheriff Bell of Southampton County, Virginia, to catch the foulmouthed Virginia bootlegger. Sheriff Bell hid just a few feet from the North Carolina–Virginia state line while my father and I hid near the still yard. In about an hour, the cursing Virginia bootlegger came whistling down the still path to the still. My father stood up and yelled, "I've got your ass now!"

The startled bootlegger ripped, "The hell you do," as he backed across the state line and started cursing at us again.

My father stood there and listened to the tirade. "If I were you I'd shut the hell up as there is a man behind you with a gun pointed about three inches from the back of your head," my father grinned and motioned toward Sheriff Bell.

At that moment, Sheriff Bell shoved the shocked bootlegger back across the state line right in front of my father, who slugged him on the right side of his face with his right fist so hard that it looked like half the bootlegger's face had caved in as he fell to the ground. "That's for all that damn cursing that you shouted at us the other day," my father angrily yelled as he reached down and yanked the bootlegger off the ground with one hand and handcuffed him. My father thanked Sheriff Bell for his help, and we walked out with the handcuffed bootlegger shuffling along between us.

In early March 1954, my father and I had just pulled up to stop at the intersection of Statesville Road and U.S. 258 when a blue-and-white 1949 Ford zoomed by heading north toward the North Carolina–Virginia state line. We were about to pull out on U.S. 258 when two North Carolina Highway Patrol cars roared by in pursuit of the two-door 1949 Ford. We quickly joined the pursuit behind the two state troopers as my father stated, "I bet that Ford is loaded with moonshine, and if he makes it across the state line, the state troopers won't follow him in Virginia."

It was obvious that the 1949 Ford was equipped with a powerful motor that made it almost uncatchable. But sometimes it did not matter how fast a car could go; it was just a matter of good luck or bad luck. In this case, it turned out to be a matter of bad luck for the unlucky moonshine runner; his thoughts of being home free if he crossed the state line were premature. When the moonshine runner was about one thousand yards south of the Virginia state line, he slammed into a five-hundred-pound black bear, killing it immediately. The impact of the collision between the moonshine runner and the black bear tore up the moonshine runner's 1949 Ford, busted his load of bootleg and broke his nose and right arm. The 1949 Ford had license tags from Virginia, South Carolina, Georgia, Tennessee and Kentucky under the visible North Carolina license tag. The moonshine runner, who was from Smithfield, North Carolina, indicated that he was headed to Newport News, Virginia, to deliver his load of stump juice.

In mid-March 1954, my father and I were checking out a report that there was a still operating off Hill's Ferry Road. We walked along the dirt road for about a quarter of a mile until we noticed a path going into the woods beside a large oak tree. We had not gone very far along the path when we began picking up the tell-tale smell of moonshine. We followed the path for about another hundred yards. We found a small still that was running, but apparently the bootlegger had heard something and vanished.

"Looks like whoever was here took off," my father said. But no sooner than my father had gotten the words out of his mouth than a four-foot-tall man peered over the rim of one of the oak mash barrels. My father immediately recognized the little man. "Stump, what in the hell are you doing out here? I would have never thought you'd be messing with this stuff."

"My wife there she needs some of them new store-bought teeth, and they're gonna cost about as much as the last mule that I bought. Running off a little moonshine is the only way I can get the money," Stump replied in a voice that sounded just like the cartoon character Elmer Fudd.

"Ouch, that'll put a big hurt on your pocket book," my father grinned. "Sorry about that, haven't seen your wife in a good while. What happened to her?"

"It's a mighty strange thing that happened to her. Never seen anything like it before. She got real sick one day, and most of her teeth just plumb fell right out of her head," Stump replied.

"My goodness, never heard of anything like that before," my father stated. "Now this is what we are going to do here today. My boy and I are going to walk out of here, and when we come back this way in a couple of months or so, you had better not be here."

"Oh, bless you, sir, I am mighty grateful for your understanding and kindness. In a couple of months, I'll be long gone outta here," Stump replied as my father and I walked away.

The last week of March 1954 found my father and I lying on a small still just off Beaver Pond Road. We had been hiding under some heavy underbrush right beside the still path for about forty-five minutes when we heard someone coming in singing "We Shall Gather at the River." The bootlegger coming in was a very tall and skinny man with a terrible gastrointestinal problem; he nearly asphyxiated us when he walked by on his way to the still. Some of the gas that he passed would have peeled the bark right off any white oak tree. When we surprised him at the still, my father asked, "What in the world have you been eating to blow you up like that?"

"My lady there, she ain't much to look at, but she shore can cook. Last night, she was real good to me. She fixed me a big mess of sweet potatoes, collards, a big dan doodle and a mess of chitlins for dinner, and I ate till I thought I was going to bust open," the bootlegger grinned.

My father laughed. "With all that high-octane gas, no wonder you were out here, as she probably kicked you out of the house."

The bootlegger giggled, "She ate more than I did and she got to tooting her horn so badly that's why I left the house and came out here."

"That's kind of bad," my father laughed. "Glad you weren't smoking when you let go like that when you walked by us or you would have blown yourself up." We tore up the still, and my father told the man to go home and not let him catch him at a still again.

Two days later, my father and I were on a raid that would turn out to be one of the most heart-wrenching cases we had experienced. The raid was just off Blue Foot Road. My father had been given a tip that a still might be located near what appeared to be an old abandoned farmhouse that was in a terrible state of disrepair with part of its roof gone and some of the glass knocked out of some of the windows. We did find a well-worn footpath leading from the back of the house into the woods. My father looked at the house and shook his head in disbelief as we began walking the path, "Don't see how anyone in the world can live in that thing."

We had walked about a half mile when we swiftly entered the still yard and found a very sad sight. The two people trying to run the small still were unlike any bootleggers we had ever encountered on any of our previous raids. The two were an elderly and feeble man who was being assisted by a boy about twelve years old who had lost his right leg from the knee down. The boy was using a homemade crutch to get around. The elderly man was smoking some rabbit tobacco in a homemade corncob pipe. The rabbit tobacco had a sweet aroma to it. Their clothes were ragged, and they were wearing what appeared to be homemade shoes that had been fashioned out of an old car tire inner tube with wooden soles. My father looked at the elderly man and asked, "Do the two of you live in that house back there?"

"Yes, suh, I know it ain't much, but that's all we got right now between us and the devil. Lost all I had in a fire a couple years ago. Some folks were kind enough to give us a few sticks of old broken-down furniture," the elderly man replied.

"Bet it gets cold in there during the winter," my father noted.

"It sure does. It gets so cold that in order to take a bath I have to go behind the stove to wash my mess," the elderly man motioned.

"My goodness, that's mighty cold. What do you live off of?" my father asked.

"We don't have hardly anything at all, but we manage somehow to get by. I gets a small gov'ment check from the army every month 'cause I was gassed real bad in that big war over there in Europe in '17 and ain't been able to do nothing ever since. The little bit we get from running off a jug or two of shine now and then sure does help us out a mighty bit," the elderly man motioned toward the still.

My father looked at the boy and asked, "How did you lose your leg, son?"

"I fell off the back of a tractor, and a disc harrow ran over my leg, cutting it so badly that it had to be taken off," the boy said.

"So sorry," my father said as he motioned toward me. "Come on let's go back to the truck. We are going to leave these folks alone. They sure ain't hurting nobody out here doing this. They are doing the very best they can to survive, and I'm not going to take that little bit from them." As we walked out of the still yard, my father reached in his pocket and handed the elderly man some money. "Here, take this and see if you can get that boy some new clothes. He shouldn't go to school looking like that. I'm going to talk to my church to see if we can't get him an artificial leg or at least a better pair of crutches."

"Thank you, sir, may the good Lord bless you and your boy and keep you both safe," the elderly man said in a very humble and appreciative voice.

"You and your grandson please be careful out here. These woods sometimes have a way of reaching out and biting you if you are not real careful," my father nodded as we walked off.

"I know exactly what you mean, sir," the elderly man nodded.

In early April 1954, my father had received information about the possibility of a still being located on a small island in the upper Meherrin River, about a thousand yards below the North Carolina–Virginia state line. I had been on the island with my father hunting a few years earlier, but neither of us had been on the island since. When we got out of the truck, we heard a loud boom, as if something had blown up, but we could not tell exactly where the boom had come from.

"What in the hell was that?" my father asked as we quietly walked down to the riverbank, eased into a small wooden fishing boat and gently began to paddle our way upriver. We had to be careful paddling, particularly to avoid hitting the sides of the boat with the boat paddles, as the noise from that would echo or reverberate through the surrounding cypress and juniper trees and alert the bootlegger. A short distance up the river, we came to a small island where we tied up beside another small, wooden fishing boat. When we stepped onshore, we noticed that a well-beaten path led from the riverbank into the interior of the island. I followed my father quietly along the still path until we reached the still yard, where we discovered where the boom noise had come from. The still yard was in shambles. Apparently the still had gotten too hot and exploded, killing the lone bootlegger in the process. The still was almost totally destroyed, and the bootlegger probably never knew what had hit him. His left arm was blown completely off, half of his head was missing and an oak mash barrel stave had impaled his chest. My father took his hat off and shook his head in disbelief.

"Damn, just look at that! Steam rigs sure do pack a hell of a punch when they blow up like that. What a horrible mess! Hell, the blast blew half of ole Buger's head right off. What a hell of a way to go. Sure hope he had gotten himself right with the Lord before all this happened. Don't want an early trumpet call like that from above anytime soon."

"Did you know him?" I asked my father.

My father shook his head in disbelief. "Yeah, I knew him for a long time. He always seemed like a nice fellow. Don't know why he was out here making shine unless he needed the money. It sure is hard to believe he died like this. Hell, he had survived several big battles of World War II but did have half of his left ear shot off as a machine gunner on a navy dive bomber during the Great Marianas Turkey Shoot in the South Pacific. That's how close he came to losing his head to a Jap bullet."

While my father and I had encountered some odd and weird situations on moonshine raids, finding the badly mangled body of the World War II veteran at the exploded still was perhaps the most gruesome and haunting event we ever ran across. We both never forgot that particular raid and seeing that man's brains splattered against some of the undamaged mash barrels and surrounding trees.

On another raid, we found a bootlegger who had a case of body odor that stunk so bad that my father made him take a dip in the nearby small creek after he told us that he could not remember the last time he had taken a bath. My father asked the bootlegger why he waited so long to take a bath. He told us that he did not take a bath during the summer because he used wasp larvae for pole fishing bait. He would run his hand through his armpit and reach up and pull down wasp nests without them stinging him.

"Damn, never heard of that before," my father growled. "Bet your wife makes you sleep outside because you stink so bad."

"Naw, naw, she don't do that 'cause she don't take no baths in the summer either," the bootlegger replied.

"Damn, that's kind of tight," my father said, shaking his head. "You sure ain't gotta worry 'bout going broke buying any soap."

"We don't buy no soap anyway. My wife makes lye soap, but about the only time we use it is in the summer when the red bugs eat our mess up. The lye soap is about the only thing that will stop all that scratching and itching," the bootlegger said.

"Gotta have some tough ass skin to wash your tail with that stuff," my father laughed.

A few days after this raid, we surprised a bootlegger who was snoring so loudly that my father commented that he bet the man probably lived alone—no woman could stand to sleep in the same bed with him snoring like a foghorn. The moonshiner told us that his snoring did not bother his wife one bit because she snored like that, too. He told us that when his wife got a full head of snoring steam going like that, it sounded like she was going to suck the walls right in on top of the two of them. He also told us that one night his mother-in-law came to spend the night but never came back after that because she could not get any sleep with both of them snoring like that.

"Bet you didn't have no problems with that," my father chuckled.

"Sure didn't. When my wife gets a full head of steam snoring the only way that I can slow her down is to stick my fingers up her nose," the bootlegger explained.

"Bet that makes her mad," my father laughed.

"Boy, it sure does. She don't like that at all. Wouldn't let me monkey 'round for a while," the bootlegger said, shaking his head.

"She cut you off? That's kind of bad," my father smiled.

The bootlegger grinned, "Yep, sure is, but it only last three or four days."

My father and I were not easily shocked by whom or what we discovered at stills, but we both were somewhat taken aback when we found a young pregnant woman dressed in a large feedbag dress and her eighty-five-year-old tennis shoe–clad grandmother running a small still just inside the North Carolina state line off Statesville Road. The grandmother told us that the still she and her granddaughter were running had been at that site for over sixty years and that she had been running it for most of those sixty years. "Making a little moonshine is the only thing that keeps my granddaughter and me out of the poorhouse," the grandmother explained.

"I understand. I sure do hate to see the two of you out here doing this, but we are not going to stop you. If you've been running a still our here for over sixty years, you probably know a little something about being in the woods," my father said, shaking his head as we walked away.

"Thank you, sir. I am most grateful. We'll be OK out here. I talk to the critters you know," the grandmother winked with a smile.

On our raids, my father and I survived knife attacks, fistfights, misfires of booby-traps, insect stings/bites and all types of weather conditions, including getting soaked to the skin numerous times. We tangled with bootleggers from Virginia, South Carolina and other locations across North Carolina. We also

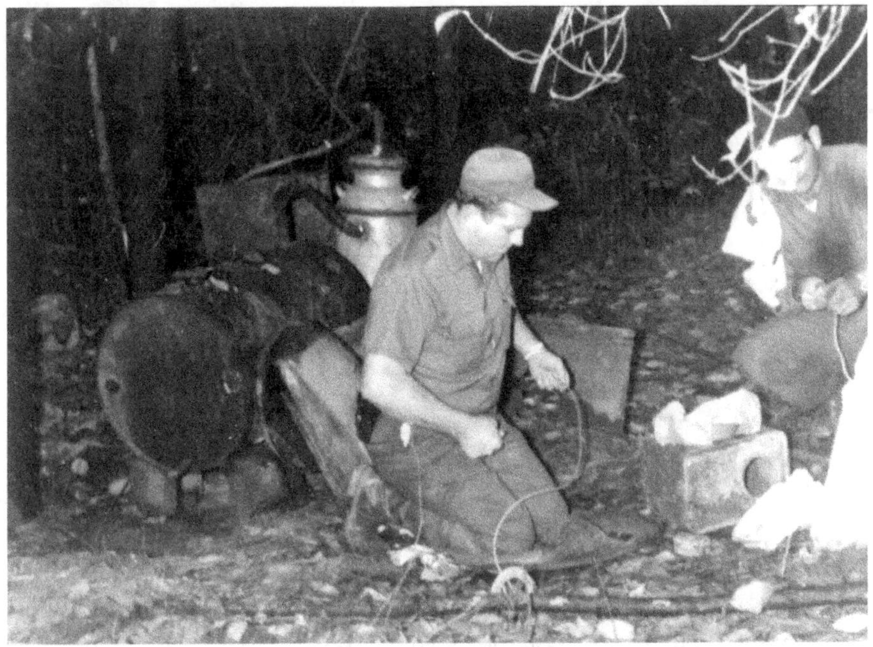

Hertford County ABC officers Calvin Pearce (*left*) and L.R. Bridges setting a dynamite charge to blow a still in the Boontown section of Gates County in 1974. *Courtesy of Calvin Pearce.*

survived being chased by a half-ton bull, attacks by dogs, bob cats, rabid fox, bats, rats and overstuffed rabbits. But none of that ever forced us to cut short a moonshine raid and leave the woods without achieving our goal. The only thing that caused us to abort a moonshine raid was, of all things, a hole of very angry ground bees. The abort happened when my father and I were on a raid off Tunis Road. I stepped in a big hole of ground bees, and they swarmed out of that hole by the hundreds and nearly ate my father and I up before we could get out of the woods and back in my father's truck. The race back to my father's truck was the fastest that I ever seen him run except on a very cold winter's day when we were chased by an angry mama hog after we had attempted to pack pine straw around her nest to prevent her newborn little porkers from freezing.

Chapter 5

Anatomy of a Tar Heel Moonshine Factory Raid

The Merry Hill Moonshine Conspiracy

The citizens of Bertie County, located in the coastal plains section of North Carolina, awoke on the morning of May 3, 1972, to find that the peaceful tranquility of their beautiful peanut-producing county had been shattered by the discovery of a jumbo moonshine still during an 11:00 p.m. raid the night before in the Merry Hill section near Midway. As news of the raid quickly spread throughout this rural county and the region, spectators by the hundreds began showing up at the site. It very quickly became obvious that this was not an ordinary illegal whiskey still. It turned out that this rig was actually a huge moonshine factory with a mash capacity of sixteen thousand gallons that had been producing almost five hundred gallons of moonshine a day. It, no doubt, was one of the largest stills ever found in the history of North Carolina. The moonshine factory was sitting beneath and behind a large mobile home located on an attractively landscaped lot that was equipped with playground equipment and a dog, giving it a deceptive family appearance of just another mobile home like hundreds of others dotting the region. This amazing moonshine factory was located in the Merry Hill section just off U.S. 17 near Salmon Creek.

News of the seizure of the Merry Hill moonshine factory created a sensation in the region as over ten thousand people would come to view the thing before it was dismantled and hauled away. People in the region almost immediately began to ask many questions, particularly, how in the world did such a thing like this find its way to Bertie County? There has been, as you might expect, a lot of speculation and stories surrounding the

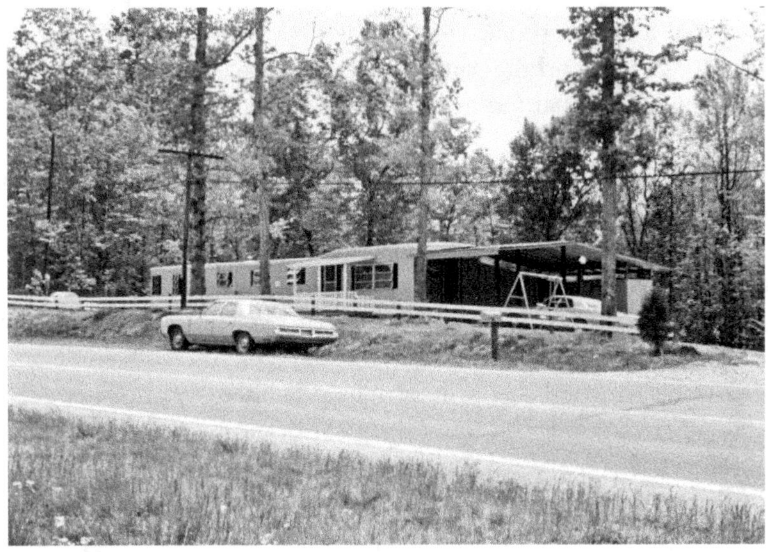

The Merry Hill moonshine factory, which was raided on May 2, 1972, by ATF and local moonshine raiders, was concealed beneath and behind this very innocent-looking house trailer. *Courtesy of Phillip McGuire.*

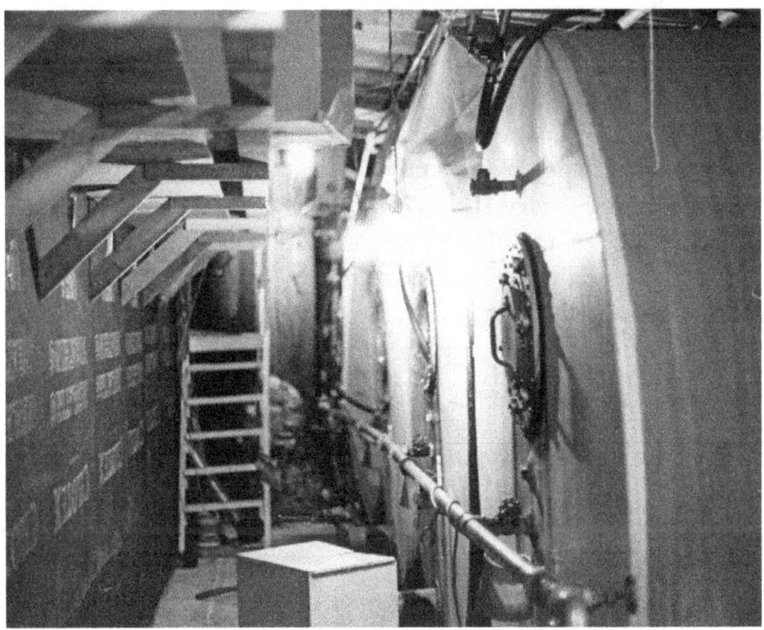

These four 4,500-gallon tanks were part of the huge moonshine factory that was raided by ATF and local moonshine raiders at Merry Hill in Bertie County on May 2, 1972. *Courtesy of Steve Barrow.*

still and how it got there and how it was discovered. Some of the stories have grown way beyond the truth while others have taken on a folklore or cult-like atmosphere that has made finding and telling the true story much more difficult.

The discovery of the huge moonshine factory at Merry Hill, North Carolina, was the result of two separate investigations going on simultaneously hundreds of miles apart. Neither of the investigations were aware that the other was underway. One of the two investigations was going on in Hertford and Bertie Counties. It began in the summer of 1971, when Hertford County ABC officer Calvin Pearce received credible information from one of his Hertford County informants that there was a very large still in operation in either lower Hertford County or Bertie County. The informant, whom Officer Pearce trusted, did not know the exact location, but he told Officer Pearce that he felt that the still was actually in Bertie County. Pearce, who firmly believed in using confidential informants and relied heavily on them, ran the information by several of his other trusted sources, who had also heard "rumblings" of a huge still in operation somewhere in Bertie County but could not pinpoint the location. After pretty much ruling out Hertford County as the location of the big rig, Pearce hooked up with agent James Saunders from the ATF office in Williamston, North Carolina, and Bertie County ABC officer Jesse Johnson. These three highly experienced moonshine raiders began an intensive search throughout Bertie County in an attempt to locate the big still. Their search would actually take them by the Merry Hill still site numerous times before the bust was finally made. In fact, Agent Saunders stated that on a number of occasions, on passing the actual still site, he felt that the site was an odd location for a house trailer, but since it appeared that a family was living there, they did not check it out. With the knowledge that a big still was supposed to be operating in Bertie County and despite the fact that they kept coming up empty-handed, the three moonshine raiders doubled their efforts to find the thing.

The second investigation was also going on in the summer of 1971 and took place primarily in western North Carolina and eastern Tennessee. It was headed by Agent Phillip McGuire, who, with other ATF agents, was conducting an investigation into an organized group of individuals who were believed to be involved in the illegal manufacture and distribution of liquor on a large scale. It was believed that the group, several of whom had a prior history of bootlegging, was operating more than one illegal distillery in western North Carolina and eastern Tennessee. This investigation would ultimately uncover the fact that the biggest still that was operating

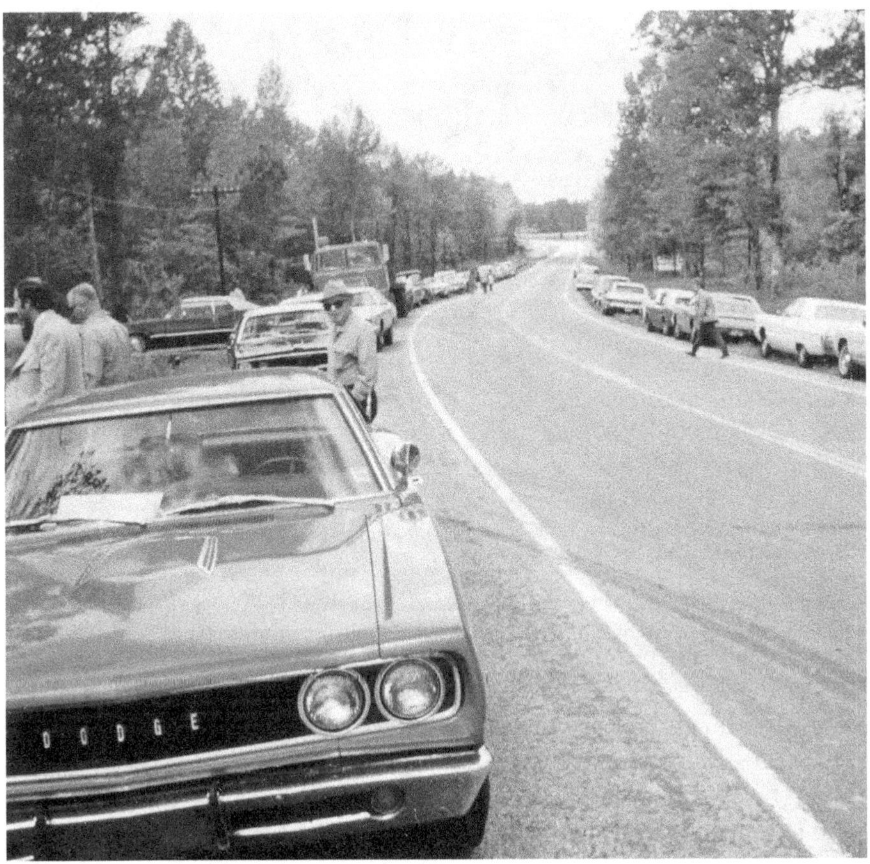

The vehicle in the left forefront was a high-speed ATF car from Atlanta. The car was used to drop off ATF agents to check out the Merry Hill moonshine factory site, which was raided on May 2, 1972. *Courtesy of Steve Barrow.*

was at Merry Hill in Bertie County, North Carolina. During the time that this group operated, from about November 20, 1970, to May 2, 1972, the evidence shows that the group fermented almost 1 million gallons of mash and manufactured 153,344 gallons of illegal and nontaxed distilled spirits at the Merry Hill still, committing tax fraud on $1,612,353.70 in revenue.

The group of moonshiners was composed of Lonless Fields of Durham, North Carolina; Hal Derrick of Dandridge, Tennessee; Julius Johnson Jr. of Winston-Salem, North Carolina; Burnett Finchum of Sevierville, Tennessee; Oscar Tapp of Rougemont, North Carolina; Paul Chambers, Eden, North Carolina; and Janice Wilson Johnson, Winston-Salem, North Carolina. Another individual from the Wilkes County region of western

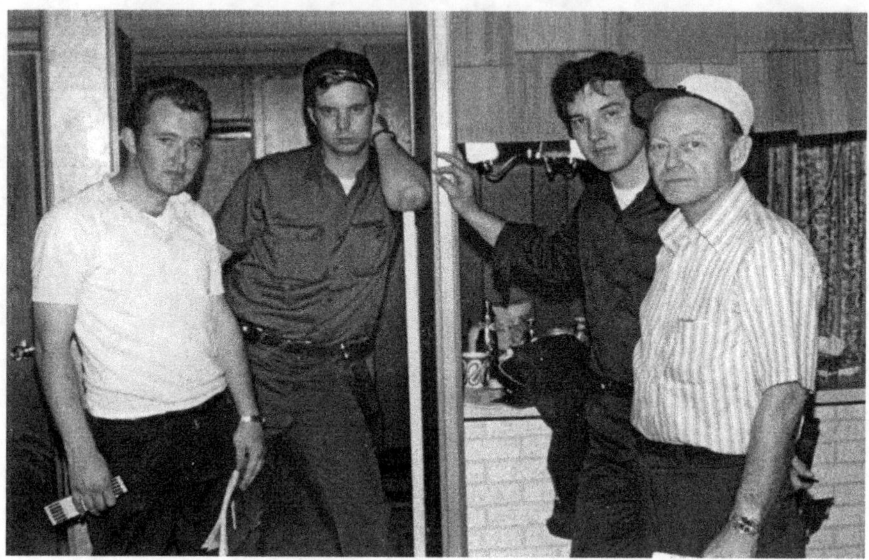

From left to right: ATF agents Phil McGuire, Steve Barrow, Neal Crisp and Don Torrence inside the house trailer that concealed the moonshine factory at Merry Hill that ATF and local moonshine raiders hit on May 2, 1972. *Courtesy of Steve Barrow.*

North Carolina was heavily involved in the conspiracy but never charged, so he will remain unnamed at this time. The unnamed individual is believed to have been the mastermind behind the design of the still and the group itself. It is further believed that this unnamed individual did not return to the Merry Hill site once the factory still was set up.

These individuals had different responsibilities for the operation. Hal Derrick and Burnett Finchum procured the raw materials and containers for the Merry Hill still. Julius Johnson Jr., Janice Wilson Johnson and an unnamed individual obtained a suitable site for the distillery and designed and furnished a clandestine cover for it. Julius Johnson Jr. and Janice Wilson Johnson also served as watchpersons for the site. Ralph Royal and Oscar Tapp were the still operators, producing hundreds of gallons of moonshine per day. Lonless Fields and Paul Chambers acquired vehicles for use in the transportation and distribution of the product.

On November 20, 1970, Julius Johnson Jr. and Janice Wilson Johnson purchased a new 1970 Madison house trailer from Oakwood Mobile Homes on High Point Road in Greensboro, North Carolina, for $10,544.40. Julius Johnson gave a North Wilkesboro, North Carolina address to the mobile home salesman and made it clear that he wanted to pick up the house trailer and not have it delivered. Sometime between November 20, 1970, and

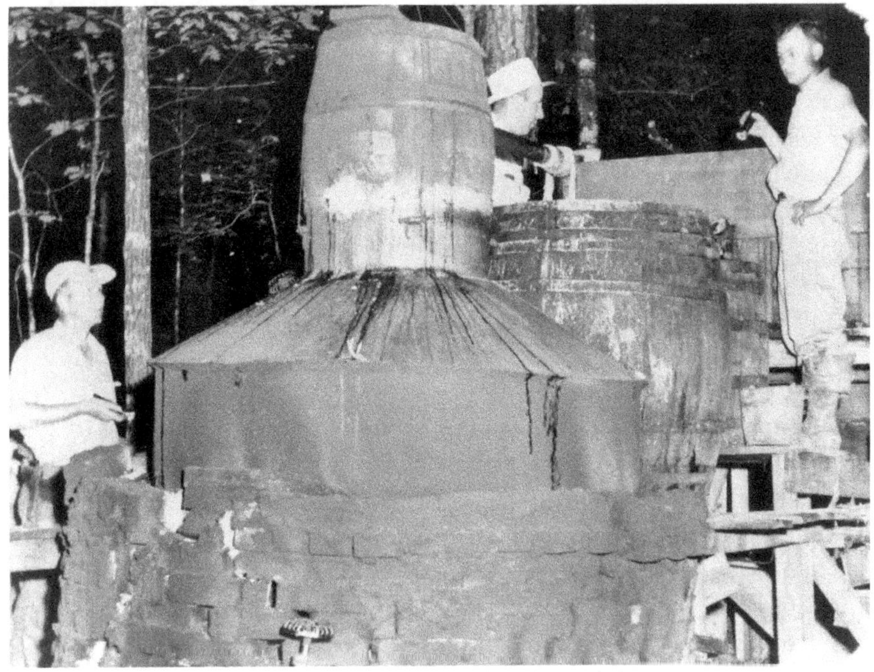

This thirty-two-thousand-gallon jumbo still was raided in July 1951 near Windsor by Bertie County sheriff Thomas Joyner and deputies. *Courtesy of Peggy J. Frisbie.*

December 8, 1970, the house trailer was picked up from a lot in Troy, North Carolina, and set up on an isolated lot in the Merry Hill section of Bertie County. On December 1, 1970, James Wilson Johnson appeared at the Roanoke Electric Membership office in Windsor, North Carolina, where he paid a $5.00 membership fee, $10.00 meter deposit and $72.00 advance payment fee. The meter was installed and activated on December 8, 1970. The lot had been leased on November 13, 1970, for a period of five years for $20.00 a month from Pauline Gillam by Julius Jackson Johnson Jr., using the name of James Wilson. In early January 1971, Julius Johnson Jr. and Janice Wilson Johnson moved into the same house trailer at Merry Hill using the names of James Wilson and Veronica Wilson. The investigation of the case would reveal that Gillam had no knowledge of the criminal intent of the person who had leased the lot from her. In fact, one of the main questions that remains unanswered today is who the local contact between Julius Johnson Jr. and Gillam was. Several names surfaced during the investigation, but the identity of the local contact has never been established.

During the early months of 1971, the Merry Hill moonshine conspirators quietly and secretly constructed the factory still behind and beneath the house trailer where Julius Jackson Johnson Jr. and Janice Marie Johnson had taken residence as James and Veronica Wilson. There remain today a number of unanswered questions surrounding the actual moving in and construction of the still. The prime question is just how did the bootleggers move such a large operation like this into this rural area without being noticed, particularly since rural folks have a tendency to be more than a little curious about activities that they are not accustomed to seeing. Perhaps we will never know the answer to that and many more questions surrounding this moonshine factory.

The construction of the still was apparently completed about the middle of April 1971 because that is when Hal Derrick approached Lee Hadad, president of Vol-Ade in Knoxville, Tennessee, concerning the purchase of large quantities of sugar. Hal Derrick and his brother-in-law, Burnett Finchum, on April 26, 1971, began their purchases with Hadad. From April 26, 1971, through April 20, 1972, Hal Derrick made thirty-nine large purchases of sugar, totaling 569,500 pounds, from Hadad.

On July 6, 1971, Hal Derrick purchased 21,600 one-gallon plastic jugs from Willian Daniels in Knoxville, Tennessee. From October 15, 1971, through April 28, 1972, Hal Derrick purchased huge quantities of one-gallon plastic jugs, totaling 82,944 jugs, from Lee Hadad.

On August 10, 1971, ATF agent Phillip McGuire contacted William Daniels regarding his association and business transactions he might have had or was having with Hal Derrick of Dandridge, Tennessee. After Agent McGuire advised Daniels of his constitutional rights, Daniels agreed to meet with Agent McGuire in the office of attorney McAfee Lee in Knoxville the next day. During the meeting on August 11, Agent McGuire questioned Daniels concerning his relationship with Hal Derrick. Daniels confirmed that he had known Hal Derrick since December 1966 and, since that time, had been selling him large quantities of one-gallon plastic jugs. Daniels further stated he was ordering the jugs for Derrick from Wursburg Brothers once a month and that this arrangement was still going on, for which Derrick was paying him $300 for each load of the jugs.

Two weeks later, on August 25, 1971, Agent McGuire, along with Special Agent D.L. Altizer, questioned Lee Hadad at his residence in Knoxville regarding his association with Hal Derrick and his brother-in-law, Burnett Wendell "Pilk" Finchum. Hadad understood his rights and agreed to cooperate, stating that he had sold Derrick large quantities of sugar over a period of months and that his association with Derrick was still going on. Agent McGuire told Hadad that he would like for him to continue his association with Derrick and make McGuire and the government aware of any and all transactions between him and Derrick. Lee Hadad agreed, with the understanding that his cooperation would play well in an attempt to avoid prosecution. Hadad was subsequently not prosecuted after ATF found the factory still at Merry Hill.

Two days later, on the afternoon of August 27, 1971, Hadad advised Agent McGuire that Derrick had contacted him regarding his intention of picking up fifteen thousand pounds of White Gold sugar later that same day. Agent McGuire, in response to the information he received from Hadad, set up observation with Agent Altizer and others at Gilbert-Hodges Warehouse in Knoxville. They observed a 1967 white Ford truck arrive at Gilbert-Hodges Warehouse. The truck, which Derrick had falsely registered to Jimmy Shipley of Morristown, Tennessee, was loaded and continued to Morristown, where it was parked on West Main Street. The truck remained parked at this location until about 9:00 p.m. on August 28, 1971, at which time the truck left and continued to Newport, Tennessee, where it parked next to the Ramada Inn just off I-40.

At 6:00 a.m. on August 29, 1971, Agent McGuire saw the 1967 white Ford truck traveling east on I-40 near the North Carolina line. At 7:30 a.m., Agent McGuire saw the truck parked on the westbound side of I-40 in North Carolina near the Tennessee state line. McGuire was not sure what was going on but would later find out from a September 14 telephone call he received from Lee Hadad. Hadad told McGuire that he had met with Derrick near Derrick's home in Sevierville County, Tennessee, where they went over the sugar sale of August 27, 1971. Derrick told Hadad that federal agents had been following them and that they had parked the truck on I-40 and had paid a wrecker $300 to pull the truck to Newport, where they watched to see if the federal agents were following it. Hadad also told Agent McGuire that Derrick wanted to purchase more sugar on September 16 and would contact him by telephone.

Agent Phillip McGuire was contacted by Lee Hadad on September 16, 1971, advising him that he, Hadad, had assisted Hal Derrick, at his request, in renting a truck from East Tennessee Fleet and Leasing Company in Knoxville. Hadad further stated that after renting the truck, he and Derrick continued to the Gilbert-Hodges Warehouse in Knoxville, where he, Hadad, purchased 12,500 pounds of White Gold sugar and sold it to Derrick. The sugar was loaded on the rental truck. Hadad further stated that after the sugar was loaded, they continued to the Vol-Ade Plant in Concord, where the sugar was unloaded and stored at Derrick's request. Hadad rented a truck for Derrick from East Tennessee Fleet Leasing on two other dates in September, the twenty-third and thirtieth. Derrick and Finchum were using the leased truck to haul sugar in an attempt to avoid detection by ATF agents who were trying to maintain surveillance on them.

On September 18, Agent McGuire was again contacted by Lee Hadad. Hadad told McGuire that Hal Derrick had met with him at the Vol-Ade Plant in Concord and that Derrick was driving the same 1967 Ford truck that belonged to Derrick. The truck had been painted green, and 12,500 pounds of White Gold sugar had been loaded on the truck and had been driven off to Hadad did not know where.

Lee Hadad contacted Agent McGuire on September 25 to inform him that Derrick had picked up another load of sugar and asked if Hadad could provide him with one-gallon plastic jugs. Hadad asked McGuire if that was permissible. Agent McGuire agreed but again reiterated to Hadad that he must keep him and the government apprised of any and all transactions. Hadad said he would. It was during this time that Hadad told McGuire that he had seen portable radios in Derrick's car and in the truck driven by Derrick and Finchum. Hadad told McGuire that Derrick had indicated to him that the radio was a monitor used to pick up and monitor police calls and "federals'" radio transmissions that would enable them to know if they were being followed.

On October 15, 1971, Agent McGuire was advised by Lee Hadad that earlier that day he had sold Hal Derrick 16,500 pounds of sugar and 2,928 one-gallon jugs. Hadad further indicated that the sugar and jugs were loaded in Derrick's green 1967 Ford truck bearing Tennessee license plates PS2676 and being driven by Finchum. Two days later, Agent McGuire, with Special Agent Neil Crisp, set up observation on I-40 west of Asheville, North Carolina. Agents McGuire and Crisp had not been on the lookout very long when they observed Derrick's 1967 Ford truck with a green cab heading east on I-40. The driver was Pilk Finchum, Hal Derrick's brother-in-law. McGuire and Crisp maintained their surveillance of the truck through Hickory, Statesville and Winston-Salem and advised ATF special agent Michael Zetts of their actions.

On December 29, 1971, and again on January 3 and 17, February 2 and 24, March 9 and 23 and April 4 and 20, 1972, Hal Derrick and Burnett Finchum rented a truck from East Tennessee Fleet and Leasing Company, using the name of Jim L. Shipley. The truck that was rented on December 29 was returned to East Tennessee Fleet and Leasing Company on December 31, 1971, with the odometer indicating that it had been driven 996 miles over the two days. The distance between Knoxville and the Merry Hill still via the Gilbert-Hodges Warehouse and the Vol-Ade Plant was the same—996 miles, as verified by Agent Phillip McGuire. On several occasions when Derrick and Finchum had used a rental truck from East Tennessee Fleet and Leasing, the trucks were returned with only 20 or 30 miles on them instead of the 996. The reason for the difference was that the odometer had been tampered with.

On July 29, 1971, and October 22, 1971, when Hal Derrick picked up sugar at Gilbert-Hodges Warehouse in Knoxville, he used the fictitious name of George Jones. On March 28, 1972, Lonless Fields of Durham, North Carolina, registered at the Holiday Inn motel in Williamston, North Carolina, using the name L.E. Allen and the home address 602 Macon Street, Asheville. Agent McGuire contacted Asheville police, who advised him that there was no resident in the city by that name. Several weeks later, on April 7, 1972, Ralph Royal purchased a 1969 Ford pickup truck with a camper shell on it. He used the name of Leon Earl Allen of Route 3, Box 65, Lot 46, Greenville.

On April 6, 1972, Agent McGuire was notified by Lee Hadad of a transaction that he had with Derrick earlier that day. Hadad had sold Derrick fifteen thousand pounds of sugar at the Gilbert-Hodges Warehouse in Knoxville, where they loaded the sugar in Derrik's rental truck. Hadad and Derrick continued to the Vol-Ade Plant in Concord, where Derrick had stored a large quantity of one-gallon jugs. When they arrived at the plant, Derrick told Hadad that there were three bags of trash and some cartons in the truck that he would like Hadad to dispose of. Hadad told Agent McGuire about the three bags of trash, telling him that he thought Derrick had brought the trash back from a distillery at an unknown location. Agent McGuire told Hadad to immediately secure the bags of trash and cartons until he could get there. When Agent McGuire inspected the three plastic bags of trash on April 10, 1972, he struck pay dirt. In addition to the empty Monsanto Jug boxes and numerous items of household trash, there were a large quantity of empty two-pound yeast cans and a catalogue addressed to James Wilson, Route 1, Box 62, Merry Hill, North Carolina.

On April 14, 1972, Agent McGuire turned the empty cardboard cartons, empty yeast cans and other trash over to Special Agent Richard Ruth to be processed for fingerprints. Two days later, on April 16, 1972, McGuire informed Special Agents Robert Martin and Henry Byrd in the Salisbury,

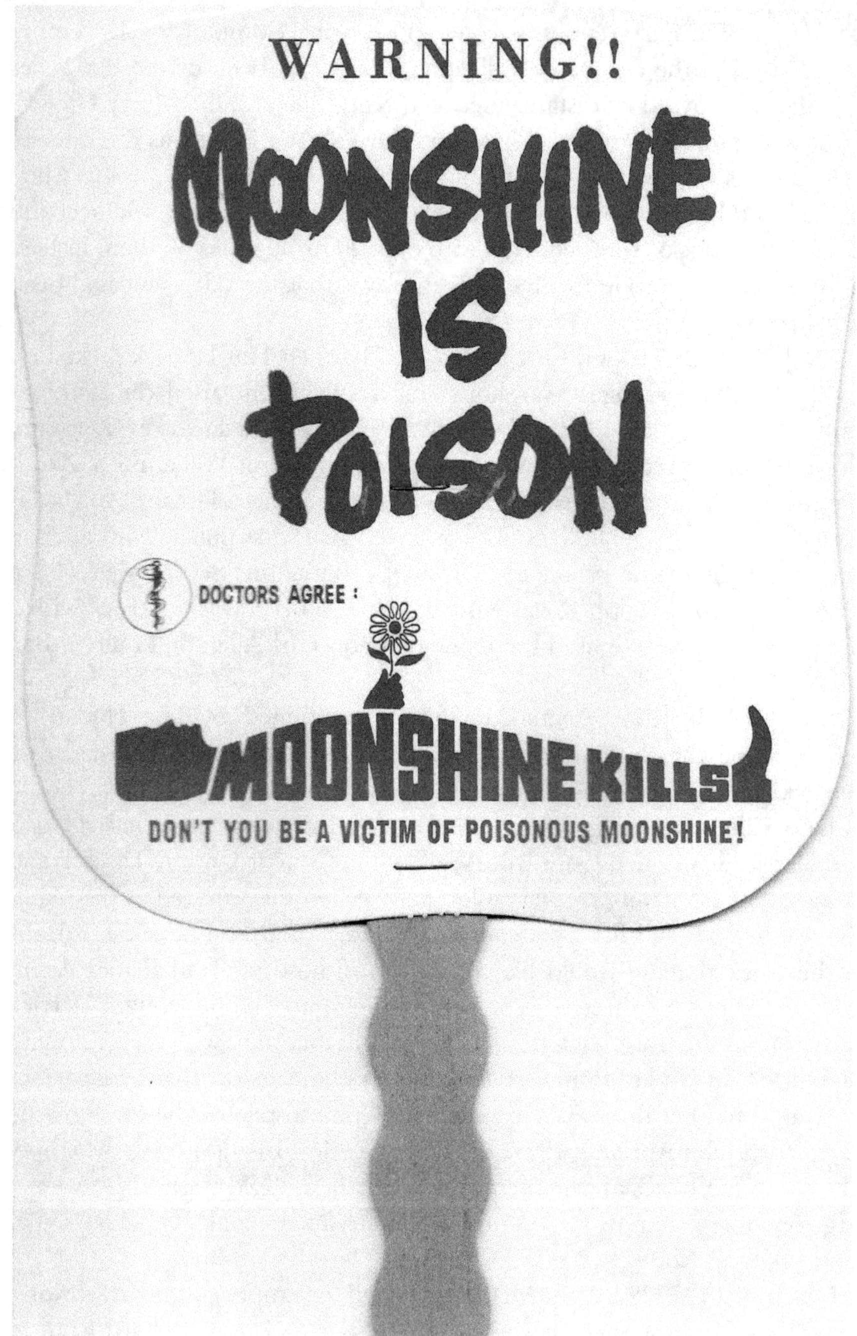

Fans like this were utilized by ATF in the fight against moonshine in North Carolina. *Courtesy of Steve Barrow.*

North Carolina ATF office of the address in Merry Hill in Bertie County. This set in motion a series of investigative events that were designed to pinpoint the exact address and to determine if it, indeed, was the location of the still in question. Agent Robert Martin contacted the ATF office in Williamston, which resulted in a meeting at the Holiday Inn there on April 17. The meeting consisted of ATF area supervisor Donald Torrence; Agents Robert Martin, James Saunders, Henry Byrd, Harry Smith, Steve Barrow and Raymond Hart; Hertford County ABC officer Calvin Pearce; and Bertie County ABC officer Jesse Johnson.

The address was quickly nailed down in the Merry Hill section, and on the night of April 17, 1972, at around 11:30 p.m., ATF agents Saunders, Martin, Byrd, Smith and Hart, along with Officer Pearce, were dropped off near the site. The agents made their way behind the large house trailer. ATF had put some extremely qualified and experienced agents on the ground, and there would be no turning back as they set up what began as a prolonged observation of the suspected site.

During the hours between 11:30 p.m. on April 17 and 4:00 a.m. on April 18, the officers heard noises coming from the house trailer that sounded like a large distillery boiler in operation. They also heard what sounded like a water pump running intermittently until around 4:00 a.m., when the noises coming from the house trailer completely stopped. At 4:10 a.m., they saw a bright light come on inside the trailer and observed two white men moving around inside. At 4:55 a.m., they observed a yellow pickup truck with a camper shell come from behind the residence. The truck appeared to be heavily loaded, and the driver did not turn on the headlights until he reached the Salmon Creek Bridge on U.S. 17, a distance of about 350 yards. At 5:00 a.m., a white Ford pickup with a camper shell and a blue Oldsmobile left the residence without their headlights on.

During their initial observation, the ATF agents discovered that the site was being guarded by a large Doberman. There were a number of suggestions made concerning how to deal with the dog. No one wanted to harm it, but no one wanted the dog to harm them or give them away to the bootleggers. So they came up with a plan and enacted it over several observation trips to the site. ATF agent Steve Barrow, who had a strong arm, tossed golf ball–size pieces of hamburger to the dog. Barrow developed such a bond with the dog that he was able to remove the dog's collar and write his initials on the underside of it. Agent Barrow did that just in case the moonshine raiders did not catch the bootleggers there and the dog showed up elsewhere. However, the presence of the large

Doberman still would have a major effect on how the raiders would play this site from here on out.

ATF continued observation on the still site, and one week later, the ATF agents, along with ABC officers Calvin Pearce and Jesse Johnson, were on the ground again near the Merry Hill still around 8:00 p.m. They moved to a point in the woods about thirty-five yards east of the trailer, where they saw a frame addition attached to the back side of the trailer. The addition was about twenty feet wide and sixty feet long. The smell of fermenting mash and the sounds of a boiler in operation were coming from the trailer and the frame addition. The moonshine raiders found an electric pump concealed in a wooden box. A plastic hose ran from the pump to the trailer. Another plastic hose ran from the trailer into the swamp behind the trailer where the slops (spent mash) from the still were being swallowed up by swamp water and the odors of the swamp.

In the meantime, Agents Saunders and McGuire began taking aerial photographs of the Merry Hill still site. Saunders used the ATF plane out of Charlotte, North Carolina, while McGuire employed a Coast Guard helicopter from Elizabeth City. Hertford County ABC officer Calvin Pearce accompanied Agent Saunders on the ATF plane out of Charlotte. Both agents, Saunders and McGuire, flew close enough to the still site to capture it on film but not close enough to spook the bootleggers.

On April 20, 1972, a party of two people registered at the Ross Motel in Williamston, using the name J.R. Minton. On the same evening, a man named Marvin B. Wiggs checked into the Ross, and during the night someone stole the license plate NC 1972VF5724 from his car. Also on the same night, L.J. Johnson, Oscar Tapp, Lonless Fields, Ralph Royal and an unnamed individual were in a 1969 Plymouth four-door sedan parked at A.H. Pierce's store on Highway 32 in Gates County, North Carolina. The car was owned by the unnamed individual (the supposed mastermind of the still operation), and its license plate was covered with damp mud, which prompted North Carolina state trooper Michael L. Harrell to walk over and check it out. Trooper Harrell found five men in the car, three in the front and two in the back. L.J. Johnson, Oscar Tapp and the unnamed member of the group were in the front. He established the real identities of the men in the front but the two in the back were actually Lonless Fields and Ralph Royal, who told Trooper Harrell that they were Roger Harris of Fayetteville and J.R. Minton of Mooresville, respectively. Trooper Harrell observed a partially visible license plate under the driver's side of the front seat. The unnamed individual told Trooper Harrell that he had seen the plate on the road and had picked it up. The license plate was the same one that Marvin Wiggs had lost. Trooper Harrell further observed that there was a Sonar brand shortwave radio monitor plugged into the cigarette lighter and a long radio antenna mounted on the trunk lid. He also noted that there were three walkie-talkie radios and some men's clothing in the car. Trooper Harrell would see three of the five occupants of the car again in the early morning hours of May 3, 1972. Two of them, Oscar Tapp and Ralph Royal, he saw in custody at about 1:00 a.m. on May 3, 1972 at the Merry Hill still. The third one he saw in the car on April 20 and again on May 3 was Lonless Fields, who was in custody at the Edenton, North Carolina police station when he arrived there around 1:30 a.m. on May 3.

It is interesting to note that the A.H. Pierce store in Gates County was located about thirty miles from the Merry Hill still. This raises the question of why these men were in Gates County in the first place. Since the Merry Hill operation seemed to be doing quite well for the group, there is some reason to believe that the men were searching for a secluded site in Gates County to set up another large still. The fact that the unnamed individual was even in the region in the first place adds considerable credence to the suggestion that the group was actively searching for another location to put down another big still. The isolation and rugged swampy landscape of Gates County would have been an ideal location for them to set up another big rig. But the question of why the group was in Gates County is one of the many surrounding this case that will probably never be answered.

At 3:00 p.m. on May 2, 1972, the ATF moonshine raiders appeared before U.S. magistrate Herbert O. Peele in Williamston, where they signed an affidavit for a search warrant of the Merry Hill moonshine factory site. The search warrant was issued and set into motion the legal authority to enter the Merry Hill still site.

At 7:10 p.m. that same day, Ralph Royal drove a 1969 green Ford pickup truck with a camper shell to a public boat landing at Eden House, North Carolina. He got into a parked blue 1967 Oldsmobile and drove off, heading west on U.S. 17 in the direction of Merry Hill, still about three miles away. At 7:13 p.m., Paul Chambers and Lonless Fields drove to the same boat landing in a blue 1969 Ford sedan with a long radio antenna in the middle of the top of the trunk lid. At 7:15 p.m., Chambers got into the 1969 Ford pickup truck and Fields returned to the 1969 Ford sedan, and both drove off on U.S. 17 toward Edenton, North Carolina. In Edenton, Fields and Chambers registered at the Eden Motel under assumed names.

After securing the federal search warrant, the ATF agents finalized their plan of attack on the Merry Hill still site. It was now time to hit the still and to find out exactly what was there. At 10:30 p.m. on May 2, 1972, a large moonshine raiding party, consisting of ATF agents James Saunders, Robert Martin, Henry Byrd, Phillip McGuire, Harry Smith, Stephen Barrow, Pern Lundell, Glenn Wojahn, Richard Ruth, Raymond Hart and Charles Stanfill; area supervisor Donald Torrence; Hertford County ABC officer Calvin Pearce; and Bertie County ABC officer Jesse Johnson, quietly made its way to the still site. The men determined that some of the bootleggers were there and that the still was in operation.

At 11:00 p.m., the moonshine raiders stormed the house trailer of James and Veronica Wilson. Agent Phillip McGuire, with Agent Steve Barrow right behind him, opened the front door and entered the trailer. At the back door, Agent Robert Martin loudly stated that he was a federal officer with a federal search warrant, and a swarm of moonshine raiders poured into the building, surprising Ralph Royal and Oscar Tapp, who were standing beside one of the big tanks. Tapp attempted to flee through the upstairs but was quickly detained by Agent Martin. The two bootleggers, Royal and Tapp, were arrested and advised of their rights.

There were no signs posted at the distillery to indicate that it had been registered, nor were there any federal stamps on the containers of moonshine as required by law. The distillery and a blue 1967 Oldsmobile sedan were immediately seized, and Agents Harry Smith and Richard Ruth lifted latent fingerprints there belonging to Ralph Royal, Oscar Tapp, Lonless Fields and Julius Johnson Jr.

When the dust had cleared, the moonshine raiders soon realized that they had busted one of the largest stills ever found in eastern North Carolina. What they had found at the Merry Hill site was not just an ordinary still but a highly sophisticated moonshine factory quite similar in design and operation to some of the giant stills found in the central and mountain regions of North Carolina and particularly in the Wilkes County region. The Merry Hill moonshine factory consisted of four 4,500-gallon tank "pot" stills with a 500-gallon high-pressure upright boiler, an 800-gallon metal doubler, a wooden cooler box, a copper multi-tube condenser, 10,000 pounds of corn meal, 720 1-gallon plastic jugs, 1,600 gallons of mash and many other items, including tools, piping, buckets and vats. One and one-half gallons of moonshine and a hand truck were also found at the still, along with a boat motor that was used to stir the mash in the 4,500-gallon tanks. The agents discovered that the bootleggers had bypassed the electric meter box by stealing electricity from REA. In addition to seizing the site (trailer and still), the moonshine raiders seized three vehicles: a 1967 Oldsmobile sedan, a 1969 Ford sedan and a 1969 Ford pickup truck.

When the Merry hill moonshine factory was seized and secured, the moonshine raiders McGuire, Saunders, Hart and Martin turned their attention to the other bootleggers who were involved at the Merry Hill still. At about 12:50 a.m. on May 3, 1972, they arrested Paul Chambers and Lonless Fields in Room 19 at the Eden Motel in Edenton. Fields was registered under the assumed name of Roger Dean Harris of Fayetteville, North Carolina. At the time of his arrest, Fields had in his possession $800 in cash and the keys to the blue 1969 Ford sedan that was parked in front of the room. The car contained the two Sonar brand shortwave radios and $1,200 in cash. One of the Sonar monitors was set on 39.1, the local radio frequency that was utilized by most North Carolina law enforcement officers. The other monitor contained two crystals for monitoring ATF frequencies, and both monitors were able to listen to radio conversations on all three frequencies utilized by the Williamston ATF office. Shortly after Fields and Chambers were arrested, the ATF raiders seized a green 1969 Ford pickup truck with a camper shell in the parking lot of Chowan Hospital in Edenton. The truck contained traces of sugar and meal, raw materials used in the manufacture of moonshine. Fields and Chambers were temporarily housed in the Edenton and Williamston city jails, respectively, pending the arrival of a U.S. magistrate.

On May 3, 1972, at about 6:00 p.m., defendants Chambers, Fields, Royal and Tapp appeared before U.S. magistrate Grafton C. Beamon in Elizabeth City. Each defendant waived preliminary hearing and was released on $500 bond for their appearance in U.S. District Court.

At 11:00 a.m. on May 10, 1972, ATF agent James Saunders obtained a federal arrest warrant from U.S. magistrate H.O. Peele in Williamston for the arrest of Janice Wilson Johnson and Julius Jackson Johnson Jr. Later that same day, at about 8:50 p.m., ATF area supervisor Queen with Agents Saunders and Hart arrested Julius Johnson Jr. and Janice Wilson Johnson at a house trailer in Winston-Salem. They were advised of their rights and taken to the ATF office in Winston-Salem, where they were fingerprinted and cited for appearance on May 11 before a U.S. magistrate. On May 11 at 11:30 a.m., Julius Johnson Jr. and Janice Wilson Johnson appeared before U.S. magistrate Eric Davis in Wilkesboro, North Carolina. Both defendants waived preliminary hearings and were released under a $500 bond for appearance in U.S. District Court.

Once the huge moonshine factory was seized, there was the obvious question of what to do with the thing. Dynamite was ruled out, but several other options were discussed. Finally, ATF contracted with Manuel Kiser of Kiser Salvage Company in Concord, North Carolina, to remove the still and its four big tanks. Kiser and his company earlier had removed another large still for ATF and had set it up near Concord as the "Moonshine Museum." Manuel Kiser agreed to remove the big rig at Merry Hill if he could add it to his moonshine museum in Concord. ATF agreed, with the understanding that they be present when the still was dismantled and disabled. On May 12, 1972, Agent Robert Martin of Salisbury, North Carolina, witnessed the disabling of the Merry Hill moonshine factory by the Kiser Salvage Company. When Manuel Kiser's salvage trucks arrived at the Merry Hill site, they were equipped with signs reading "White Lightning Express and Million Dollar Year Moonshine Operation."

On July 12, 1972, ATF agents Phillip McGuire and Douglas Altizer executed a federal search warrant on the Hal Derrick premises in Dandridge, Tennessee. The two agents located Derrick there and arrested him under the authority of a federal arrest warrant.

On January 23, 1973, a true bill of indictment was returned by a federal grand jury in Washington, North Carolina, against Lonless Fields, Hal Derrick, Ralph Royal, Julius Johnson Jr., Burnett Finchum, Oscar Tapp and Paul Chambers. William Daniels, Lee Hadad and Janice Wilson Johnson were not indicated by the federal grand jury. On February 13, 1973, federal arrest warrants were issued for the seven men indicated by the federal grand jury. A bond of $2,500 was recommended with a 10 percent cash deposit. A jury trial was held in federal court in Washington on October 2, 3, 4, 5 and 9, 1973, for Paul Chambers, Lonless Fields, Hal Derrick, Ralph Royal, Julius Johnson Jr. and Burnett Finchum. Tapp, Royal, Johnson, Finchum and Derrick were found guilty while Paul Chambers was found not guilty. Oscar Tapp was sentenced to a five-year active sentence with credit for time served. Lonless Fields was sentenced to five years of active sentence with credit for time served and ordered to pay a fine of $5,000. Hal Derrick was sentenced to five years of active sentence with credit for time served and ordered to pay a fine of $10,000. Ralph Royal was sentenced to five years with credit for time served. Julius Johnson Jr. was sentenced to five years and five years on probation. On October 10, 1973, Fields, Johnson, Royal, Tapp, Derrick and Finchum filed a notice of appeal from a conviction on October 10, 1973, in the U.S. Federal Court for the Eastern District of North Carolina, Washington Division. In 1974 and 1975, federal judge John

L. Larkins signed papers suspending the active sentences of the defendants and placing them on probation for a period of five years.

The solid detective work by a combined force of over thirty ATF agents and Hertford County ABC officer Calvin Pearce and Bertie County ABC officer Jesse Johnson led to the execution of the highly successful raid on the Merry Hill moonshine factory. The Merry Hill moonshine factory was the largest of five big stills that were operated by a group of bootleggers from western North Carolina and eastern Tennessee. The talented moonshine raiders who captured the Merry Hill moonshine factory described the still as the most elaborate and complicated distillery they had ever seen. The professionalism and brilliant work of these tough, smart and fearless officers drew the praise of John Wursele, the highest-ranking ATF officer to visit the Merry Hill moonshine factory. Wursele estimated that the tax loss to the federal government was over $750,000. The federal government sold the vehicles and most of the items that ATF agents seized during the Merry Hill moonshine raid, with the exception of the still itself, which was removed from the site by Manuel Kiser. As far as the Merry Hill moonshine factory site itself, today it is all grown over, providing little or no clues to what happened there over forty-five years ago.

Chapter 6

Disappearance of a Way of Life and Culture

The illegal manufacture of corn whiskey in North Carolina was a very big business for a long time. Stills of all types and sizes were found for many years in just about every nook and cranny of the state and just about anywhere you can imagine. The people who made moonshine in North Carolina also were as diverse as the stills that they operated or financed. North Carolina moonshiners ranged from the very wealthy to folks who depended on running off a few gallons a week for their very financial survival. Most anyone who resided in North Carolina during its moonshine years knew where there was a whiskey still located or knew someone who made it, ran it, sponsored it, drank it or got caught up in it by design or by accident.

One classic case of accidental association with moonshine happened in 1958, when a big-name state politician one night mistakenly stopped at an eastern North Carolina roadhouse thinking that it was a restaurant. The case really involved the politician stopping at the wrong place at the wrong time because shortly after the politician entered the roadhouse, it was raided by local officers searching for moonshine and evidence of prostitution. The raid resulted in several prostitution-related arrests, the seizure of fourteen gallons of moonshine and the discovery of a small still that was located in the woods behind the roadhouse. When the local newspaper published a story about the raid, it mistakenly listed the politician as one of the persons who was caught. Although the politician was not charged for any offense during the raid, it left him with the embarrassing task of trying to explain his

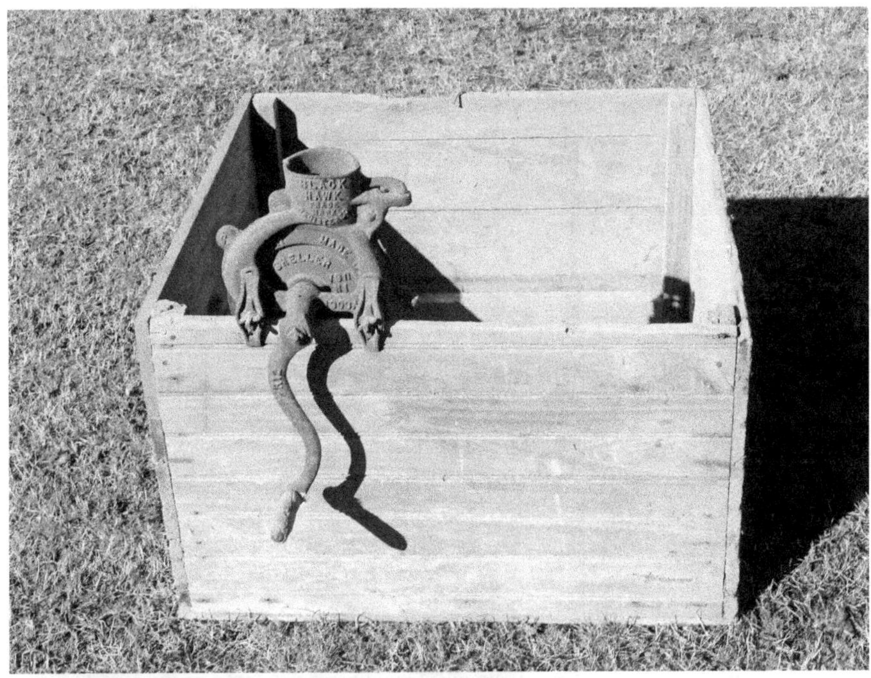

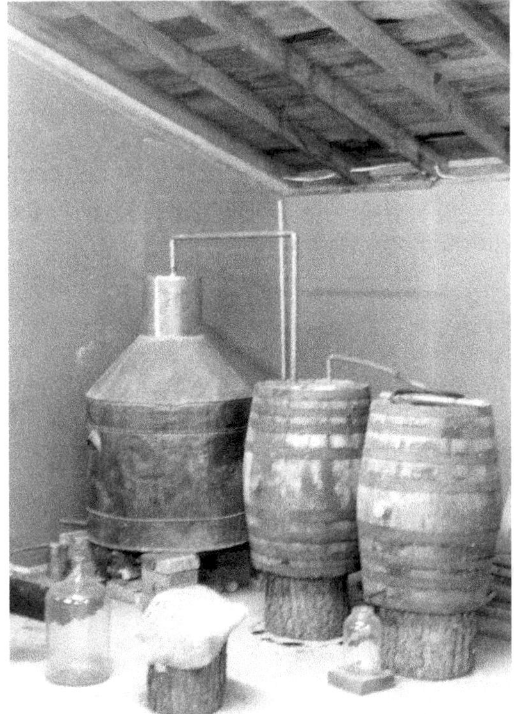

Above: This corn sheller box is a recycled large moonshine mash vat that was captured in a December 1953 raid by Hertford County deputy Frank Stephenson Sr.; his son, Frank Stephenson Jr.; and crew. The box shown here is half its original size and was one of thirty such vats that were found at the large still that belonged to a group of Virginia bootleggers. *Photograph by Caroline Stephenson.*

Left: A few museums across North Carolina have an authentic moonshine still as part of their exhibits collection. This working still is on display at the Agricultural and Farm Life Museum in Murfreesboro. Hertford County ABC officer Calvin Pearce captured and donated the still to the Murfreesboro Historical Association. *Photograph by Frank Stephenson Jr.*

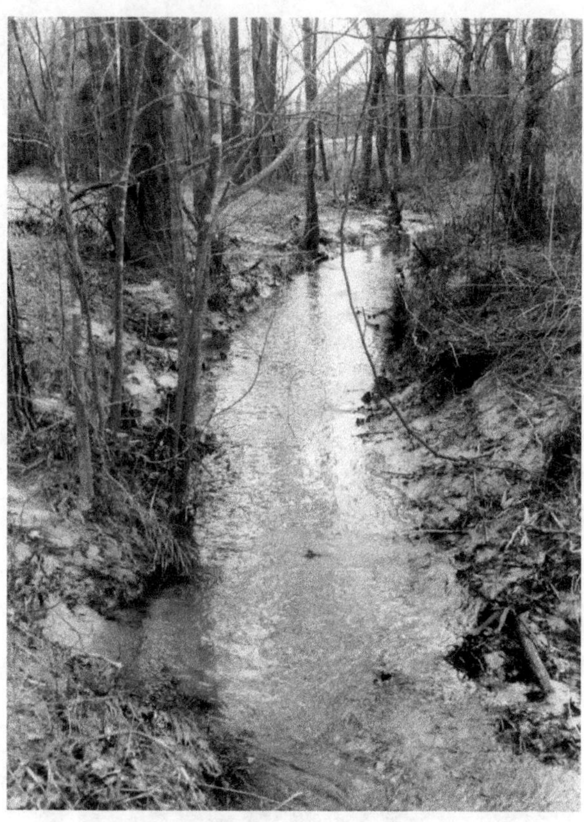
A water source for moonshine stills—a steady flow of water is working its way through this branch. *Photograph by Frank Stephenson Jr.*

presence at the roadhouse to his family and supporters. The angry politician never forgave the local newspaper and several times threatened to sue it and the reporter who wrote the story for the reporting error.

It remains a mystery today as to why legions of North Carolinians consumed huge quantities of moonshine over the years in the first place, particularly since it could be dangerous to one's health and the taste of it varied. A veteran Randolph County moonshine drinker stated that moonshine could run the taste table from "smooth as silk to burnt castor oil to eating a mouthful of fire ants." A Pitt County moonshine drinker stated that the thing that made rotgut so attractive was "the fact that no two runs of it ever tasted the same."

When narcotics began to overtake moonshine as the dominate illegal drug in the third and fourth quarters of the twentieth century, it not only spelled the end of a very colorful era but it was the beginning of the end of a unique way of life and culture that was deeply engrained in the very fabric of North Carolina. The gradual disappearance of moonshine was also fueled by the opening of state Alcoholic Beverage Control stores all across North Carolina.

Across North Carolina probably the only persons who took note of the death of moonshine as a way of life and culture primarily were the moonshine raiders and the moonshiners themselves. When moonshine began to fade, the moonshine raiders turned their attention to illegal drug dealers who, in many cases, are more dangerous and violent than most bootleggers ever were. Many of the smaller bootleggers across North Carolina were decent, God-fearing men who were trying to put food on the table and to clothe and house their families. One veteran Anson County moonshine raider noted that he knew a number of small bootleggers with large families who sent their children to school, and making bootleg was the only way they could afford to do that. The veteran moonshine raider further stated that as long as they kept their children in school and stayed out of trouble, he left them alone. Most of the bootleggers whom this particular veteran moonshine raider was referring to were very small operators, probably running off twenty-five to fifty gallons of stump juice a week. When it came to the moonshiners who were producing white lightning in large quantities, he had no mercy. Many of North Carolina's other veteran moonshine raiders also operated by the same creed.

While bootlegging as we once knew it is a thing of the past, its history and lore remain a part of our lives and will no doubt be passed on generation to generation through many diverse tales. The woods, swamps, hills and hollers of North Carolina, except for a rare case, are now void of the sounds of moonshine stills in operation. These lost sounds include the hissing of steam, the thumping of a still with a bad knock, the gurgling of water and the thud of a stir paddle on the sides of a mash barrel as bootleggers mashed up for another run. The end of the moonshine era also brought an end to the melodic sounds coming from North Carolina roadhouses, shot houses and nip joints where "Moonshine Blues" by Little Walter, "Joy Juice" by Dinah Washington and "Daddy's Moonshine Still" by Dolly Parton were often heard. Many of these establishments have long since closed and all but vanished from the state's landscape, but they were a vital part of North Carolina's vibrant moonshine history, particularly in the sale of bootleg. Earl Outland, a Northampton County deputy and ABC officer, in an interview with Frank Stephenson, said, "Moon's shot house in Roanoke Rapids sold so many ten cent shots of moonshine that the owner was able to save enough dimes to buy a new car, a Studebaker, which he paid for with dimes."

The demise of moonshine in North Carolina as a fairly easy source of revenue represented a huge setback for untold numbers of people across

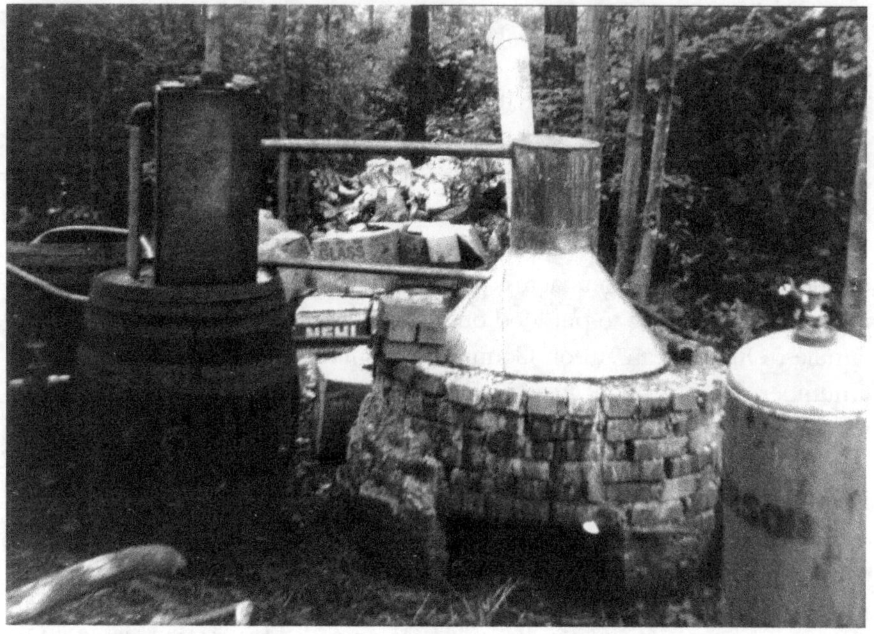

In July 1965, James Saunders and other ATF agents hit this masonry still in Bertie County. The rig was fired by propane gas and was of a design not often found in eastern North Carolina. *Courtesy of James Saunders.*

the state. Moonshine markets across North Carolina were slowly drying up, which was forcing a change in the lives of moonshiners and also greatly affected their families from a monetary standpoint. Small-time bootleggers who depended on moonshine to support their families were hit particularly hard. What did the former bootleggers do to compensate for this loss of income? A few continued to make bootleg whiskey at a huge risk while others switched over to illegal drugs. A few bootleggers used their moonshine experiences and notoriety to make a legal living.

In an interview with Frank Stephenson, a retired Bertie County moonshiner recalled his years of making bootleg before the golden era of North Carolina moonshine ended.

> *Let's see did I ever make any bootleg likker? To tell you the truth, I don't remember not making it because when I got big enough I would help my daddy at his still toting water and mashing up. For years and years, he ran a still and never got caught because he had his still hidden so deep in Indian Woods that no one outside him and me knew where the thing was. My daddy he sure could make good bootleg, and he taught me how to make good*

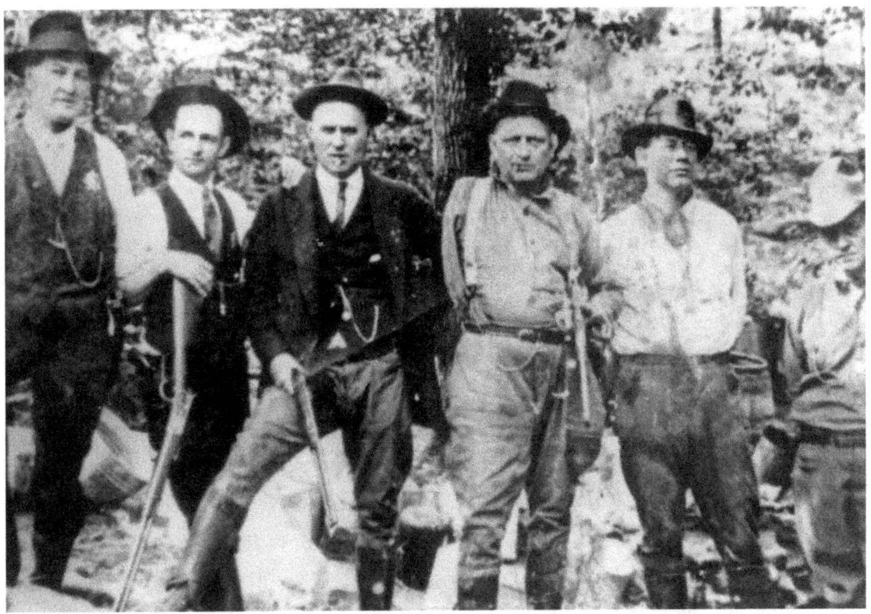

In 1921, this group of moonshine raiders hit a still in the Mount Gould section of Bertie County. *Courtesy of Bill Park.*

> *stuff just as his daddy had taught him and his daddy before him. Good moonshine is not hard to make if you know what you are doing and look after it yourself. A number of folks told me that mine was the best they had ever drunk. One man told me my shine was so good that when he ran out of gas for his old lawn mower, he poured some of my stuff in it and the mower ran like a Swiss watch. My father and his father never got caught, and neither did I. And I guess I ran whiskey for over forty years, but I had several close calls. The closest call I had was one night, the law came up quickly on me at my still. They were on me so fast that I just barely got away. They were so close behind me that there was no way I could outrun them, so I climbed up this big white oak tree without them seeing where I went. I stayed up there all night and climbed down the next morning and went home.*

Stephenson had an opportunity to sit down with a Durham man who had not made moonshine but was a likker hauler for over forty years.

> *Yeah, I was a likker hauler, and man, did I ever haul it from northern Durham to D.C., Baltimore, Philadelphia and a few other places, mainly*

> *up north. I even hauled a couple of loads up to Chicago and Detroit. That '49 Ford I had with that big modified engine in it could really roll. That was a tough damn car. The ole boy who worked on the motor in that car sure was way ahead of his time. I'd take Club Boulevard over to U.S. 1 up to 158 and slide across to 301 and roll on up north and leave anything that fell in behind me. Hell, the "Man," he couldn't even keep up with my taillights, particularly when I pushed that overdrive button in that Ford and it looked like it wanted to fly. Shoot, those big fancy race car drivers, they didn't have squat over on me as I could run with the best of 'em.*

A retired Northampton County bootlegger remembered his many years of making stump juice in an interview with Stephenson.

> *The law they never did catch me at my still. They tried many times and some of them were pretty fast, but I was just a step or two faster—that's why they called me Lightning. They ran down one of my boys back in the '60s, but they never were fast enough to catch me. One night when they raided my still, I turned the tables on them by chaining one of their cars to a large pine tree where the car was backed up to. When they finally left,*

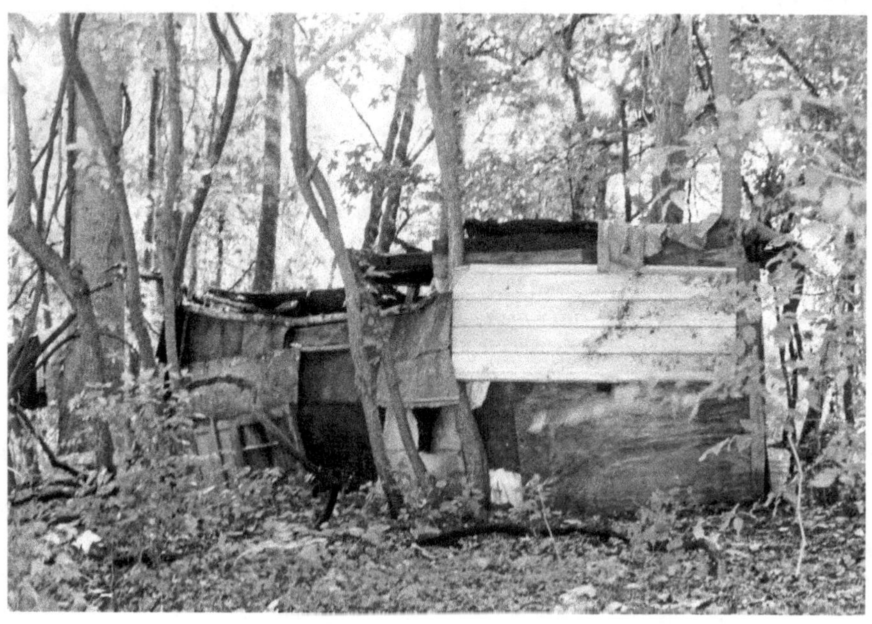

This still was located in the Great Dismal Swamp in the northern part of Pasquotank County. *Photographed by Frank Stephenson Jr.*

> *they tore the rear bumper off the car, which made them mad as a bunch of hornets! I can hear them cursing and carrying on about it right now. I sure do miss running off a jug now and then, but I can still get some pretty good stuff 'round here if I need it. It's just sad to see it all go like it has.*

In a lengthy interview with Stephenson, a Warren County bootlegger recalled his years of making and hauling bootleg whiskey.

> *I shore did make it and a lot of it, and I am proud as hell that I did. I sent all three of my children to college on the money that I made off moonshine. If I had not made shine I would have not been able to send them to get their education. I would be making it right now if I could do what I could do years ago....Making moonshine is damn hard work and I am way too old to be doing that anymore. I had a small rig just off U.S. 1 between Norlina and Wise, and I could just shoot straight up to Petersburg and Richmond, where I sold all that I could make as those Virginia folks they just loved my stuff.*
>
> *Did I ever have any close calls with the law? I had one or two. One close call was in 1959 or 1960, when the law was chasing this man from Virginia who had robbed a bank in Henderson. I had just left Wise with a load of likker, and the law, they had this road block setup on U.S. 1 just below the Virginia state line. I thought sure they were going to search my car, but they waved me on through.*

A Gates County bootlegger shared his recollections of making moonshine in a lengthy interview with Stephenson.

> *I might have run a jig or two off, but I say I might have but that doesn't mean that I really did if you know what I mean. Mostly what I ran off was for my own use, but I did run off a little bitty bit for a few close friends but never charged them anything for it. You know when you wake up in the morning feeling bad and all gummed up and no good with your head the size of pumpkin and about to blow up, just take a little sip or two of shine and by noontime all of your ailments will be long gone. I remember one time when the mosquitoes and deer flies were so bad that I rubbed a little of my stuff on my neck, arms and legs, and they didn't bother me no more. Another time I got stung on the arm by one of those nasty black wasps, and I poured some of my shine on it, and it took the fire right out of that thing. Sometimes when it is really hot in the summer I get this rash like stuff near my manhood, and I*

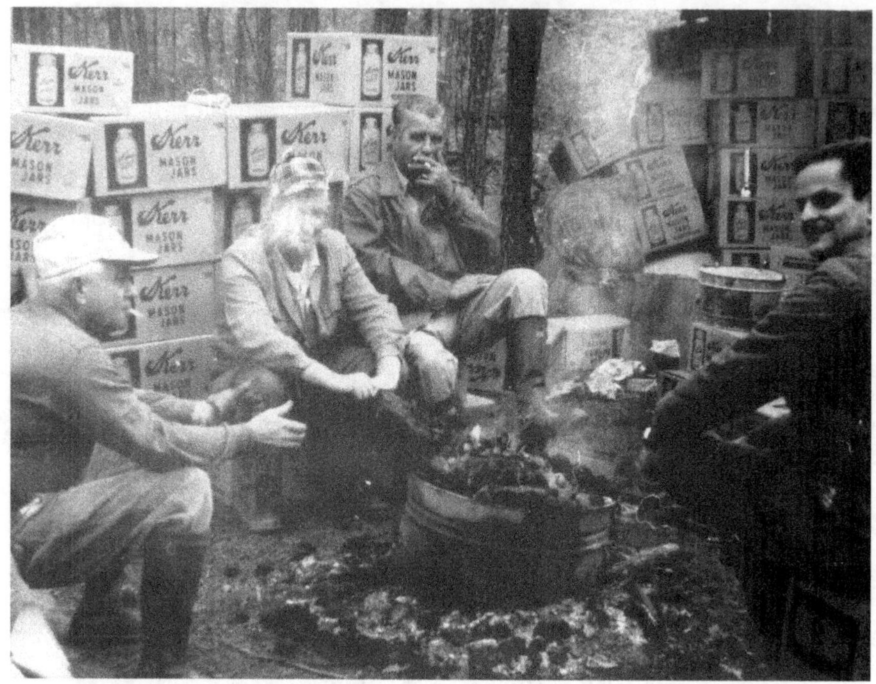

Moonshine raiders are enjoying a few minutes of camaraderie in the still yard of a huge still that ATF, local and state raiders hit near Murfreesboro in October 1960. *From left to right*: Pasquotank ABC officer Benny Halstead, Chowan County ABC officer Troy Toppin, Perquimans County ABC officer A.D. Baum and ATF agent Joseph Kopka. *Courtesy of Joseph Kopka.*

> *rub a little shine on it and it dries it right up. The law they'd bust up my little mess a lotta times, but it* [wouldn't be] *long before I had another one put down. Sometimes I put it right back in the same spot of the one they busted up. They chased me all over Buckland, but I managed somehow to stay a step or two ahead of them. I suppose I made likker for nearly fifty years, finally giving it up when the state stores came in and folks started buying or growing that dope stuff. So far as I know, nobody ever got sick or died from any of the likker I made. Shore is a terrible shame that it is all gone now. I sure could stand a drink of some good shine right now.*

One of the professions that were affected by the demise of moonshine in North Carolina was the legal profession, as bootleggers facing moonshine-related charges relied heavily on lawyers to keep them out of jail. A retired Hertford County bootlegger in an interview with Stephenson described his experience with the late Thomas L. Jones Sr., a Murfreesboro attorney.

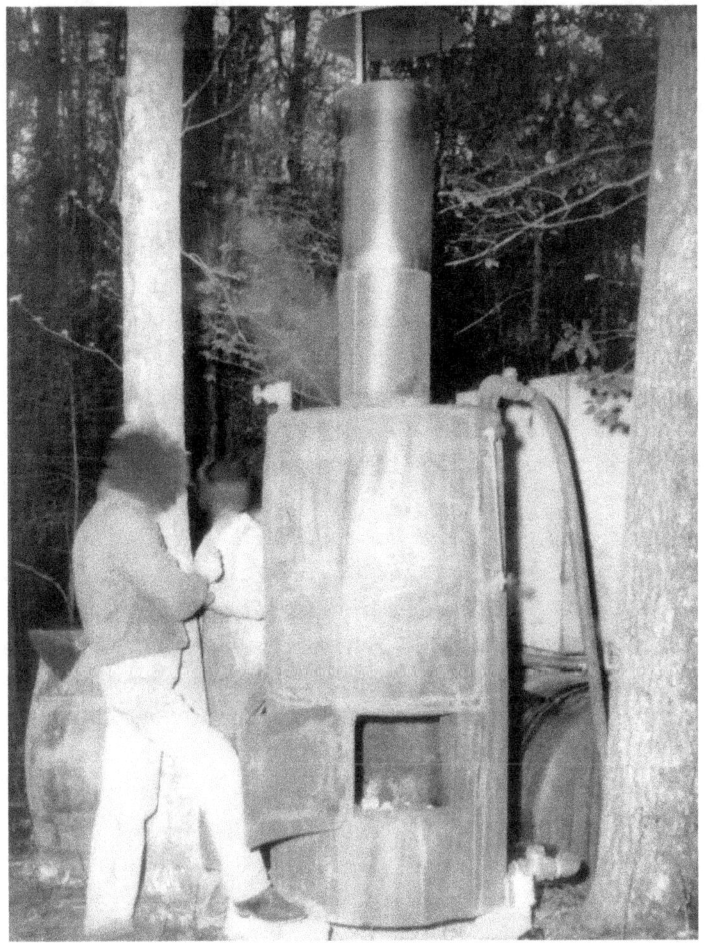

Two bootleggers found themselves in an odd predicament of being handcuffed to a tree after being caught in a raid near Gaston in 1964 by Northampton deputy Ed Ingram. The still was one of the larger ones found in Northampton County. *Courtesy of Ed Ingram.*

You know not everybody could make good likker. People who drank mine always said that I had some of the best they ever put to their lips, and I always felt that I could make some good stuff. As time went on it became harder and harder to make likker because of the sugar limit and the law becoming better and better at busting up my mess. I sure did have some close calls before they finally caught up with me. One call was so close that one night when they raided my still I was hiding in the bushes near my still when one of them stepped on my hand and never knew it. The law who stepped on my hand he...he was a pretty [NOTE: big?] fellow and I thought sure he had broke my hand. He made me mad as hell when he stepped on my hand as he must've stepped in some bear shit or som'ing and got that mess all over my hand. I thought I would never git that stinking smell off my hand.

The day they caught me it was pouring down rain, and I wasn't paying attention like I should've and did not hear them until they were on top of me and one of them stuck a gun up my nose. He sure thought he was a big shit in a shithouse when he stuck that damn cannon in my face. That was in 1957, and that thing scared me so bad that I accidently pissed on myself. The law, they took me down to Winton and locked me up in that old jail with a couple of drunks who smelled so bad that I nearly threw up all over them. I don't think they were from round here as I had never seen them before. Not only did they stink up the jail but they were some of the nastiest and ugliest folks I have ever seen in my life. Their breath stunk so bad that it is a wonder that it did not peel the paint right off the walls of the jail. I sure don't know where they came from. But I did not stay in jail very long as I got Lawyer Tom Jones in Murfreesboro to help me with my legal problems. I sure was glad to get out of that jail cell with those stinking ugly men. I can still smell them right now. Lawyer Jones he got me out of jail and went to court with me. The judge, he had a reputation for being hard and wanted to give me some time, but Lawyer Jones talked with him and saved me from going back to jail. I am so thankful to this day for what Lawyer Jones did for me. My daddy was living at that time, and he always told me that if I got in trouble and needed a lawyer to call Mr. Jones as he was the best around here.

Murfreesboro attorney Thomas L. Jones Sr. was a native of Winton and a graduate of Wake Forest College and its law school. He was a veteran of World War II and many legal battles of all descriptions. Jones represented well over one hundred bootleggers through the years and was very proud of the fact that none of them ever served any time in jail after he took their case. Jones died in 2016.

Many of the moonshine raiders who worked all across North Carolina through the years toiled in some pretty tough conditions without any special recognition except for knowing that they did their job well, and at the end of the day, they could take a great deal of pride in their work. Calvin Pearce, a Hertford County moonshine raider, in an interview with Stephenson Jr. summed up the feelings of a number of the state's moonshine raiders:

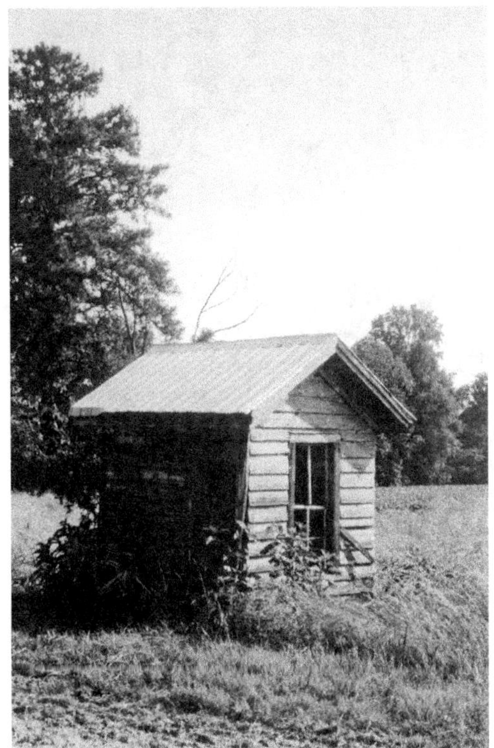

Left: A Hertford County moonshiner hid his small still in this outdoor toilet. *Photograph by Frank Stephenson Jr.*

Below: In August 1967, Hertford County sheriff R.V. Parker and crew poured moonshine in the gutter in front of the Hertford County Courthouse in Winton. The bootleg ran down the gutter into the Chowan River, where it was recycled. *Courtesy of Frank Stephenson Jr.*

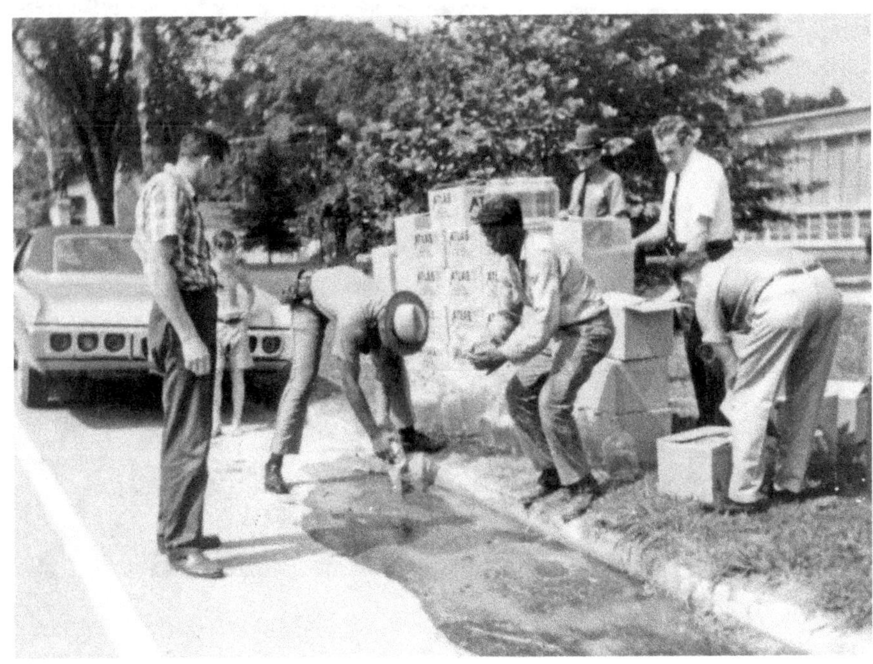

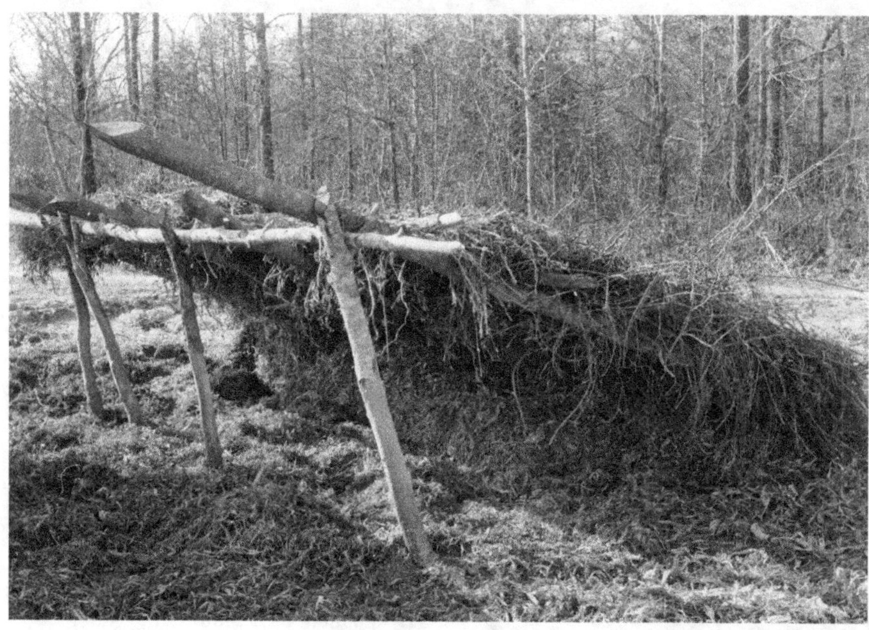

This hog shelter was used by a Wayne County bootlegger to disguise the entrance to a small underground still. *Courtesy of Frank Stephenson Jr.*

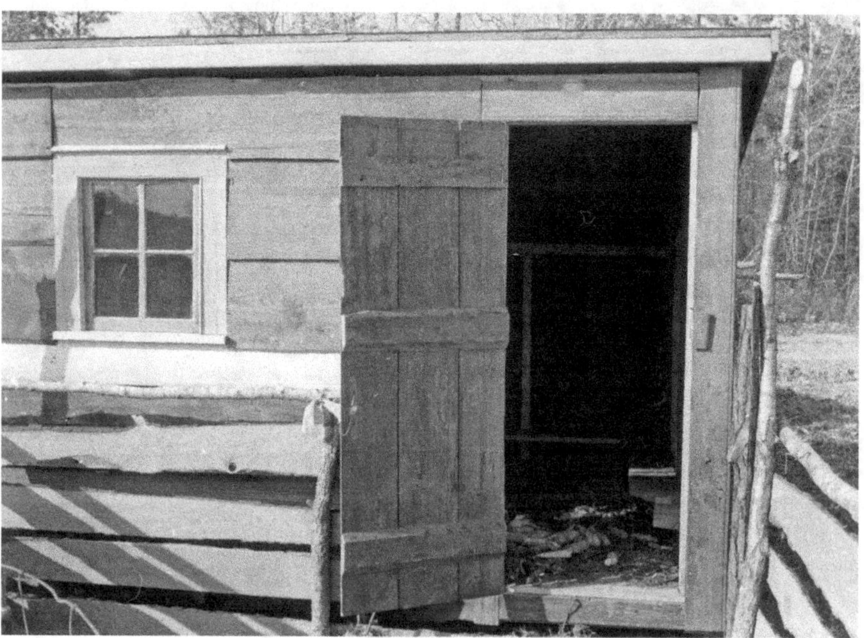

A Granville County bootlegger used this chicken house to hide his stash of moonshine. *Courtesy of Frank Stephenson Jr.*

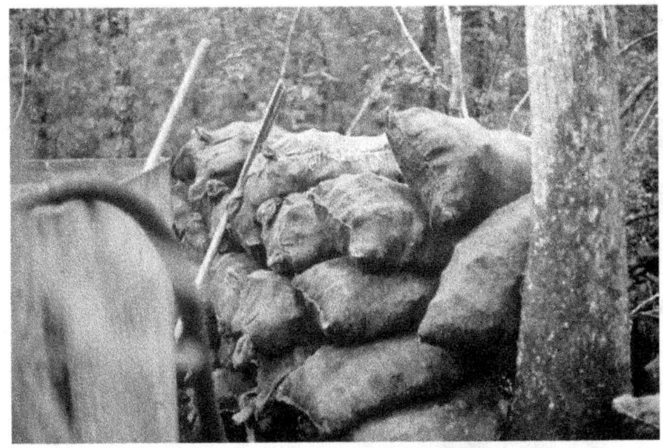

Bags of coke used to fire a still in Northampton County in the 1970s. *Courtesy of Edward Garrison.*

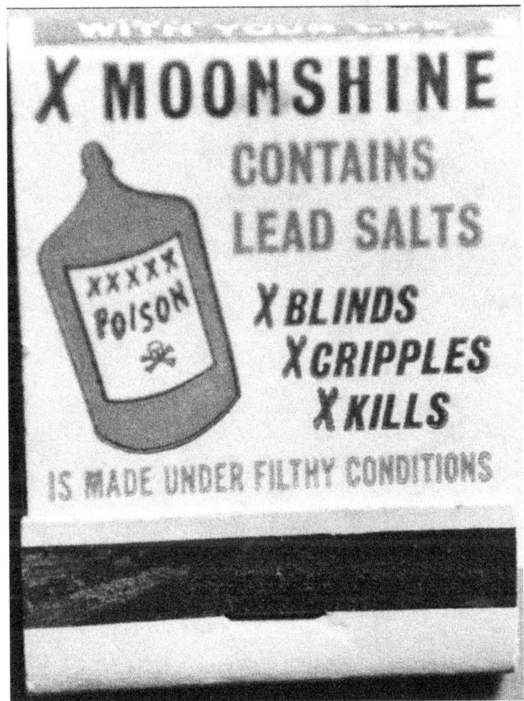

This matchbook was one of the weapons ATF used to fight moonshine in North Carolina. *Courtesy of Phillip McGuire.*

I saw many strange things during my years of busting stills, as you never knew what you might find or encounter on raids. You had to be prepared for just about anything, like when I nearly gave away my position one warm afternoon when I saw this Gates County bootlegger get his still fired up and then took a skinny dip in nearby Somerton Creek. He was most surprised when I walked up on the creek bank with his clothes in one hand and a pistol in the other. Most of the time we had the element of surprise with us and that really worked well to our advantage.

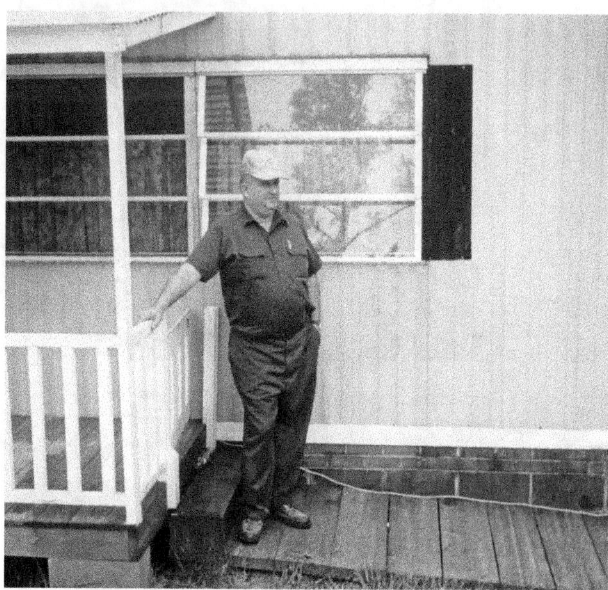

Right: Halifax County ABC officer Garland Bunting wore many disguises in his long career as a hardnosed and fearless moonshine raider for over thirty-five years. He became one of North Carolina's most famous moonshine raiders and was the subject of magazine articles and the book *Moonshine: A Life in Pursuit of White Liquor* by Alex Wilkerson in 1986. Bunting is seen here visiting the Merry Hill moonshine factory in Bertie County on May 3, 1972. *Courtesy of Steve Barrow.*

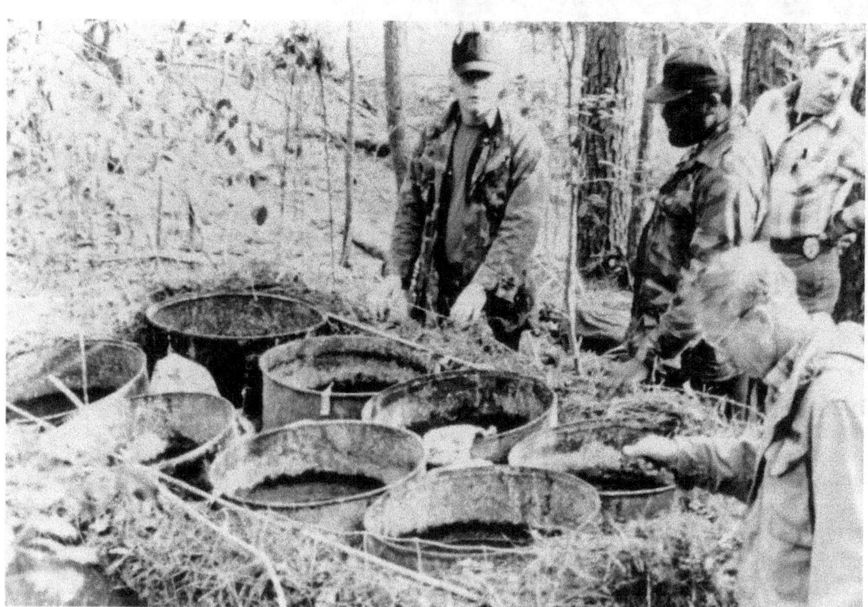

Winterize your still. North Carolina ALE officers Ken Dover and Ellis Paul, along with two Virginia ABC officers, in April 1986 raided this winterized still in Gates County. In cool or cold weather, pine straw was packed around mash barrels to increase the rate of fermentation. *Courtesy of Ken Dover.*

The state's moonshine raiders all had a common thread linking them that is best described by retired Northampton County ABC officer Ted Sumner: "Yep, there's no two ways about it, busting up stills was just one of those things that got all mired up in your blood, and you couldn't get it out if you wanted to. I'd rather bust up stills than eat when I'm hungry or do anything else that I know of!"

Moonshine was a part of the rural southern experience in North Carolina as much as apple pie, chitlins and collards. In one sense, it is sad to see it all come to an end because moonshine and its many sidebars was one of the things that made North Carolina an interesting place to live and work.

CHAPTER 7

NORTH CAROLINA'S NEW MOONSHINE

According to the North Carolina Distillers Association, there has been an explosion of new distilleries and breweries across North Carolina during the past ten years. The association estimates that there are over 150 breweries and distilleries operating in the state today, and more are scheduled to open. This revival of distilleries and brewers is not limited to one section of the state. These new alcohol-based businesses are found from the coast to the mountains and in numerous locations in between. Many North Carolina distillers are part of North Carolina's Craft Distillers Trail, which is a partnership between the North Carolina Distillers Association and the North Carolina Department of Agriculture and Consumer Services.

The Call Family Distillers of Wilkesboro in Wilkes County is an outstanding example of this rebirth or revival of moonshine in North Carolina. This is most appropriate, as the Call family's roots and heritage with moonshine extend far back in the moonshine history of North Carolina and Tennessee for at least seven generations. In Tennessee, the Call family was instrumental in the early development of the Jack Daniel's Distillery in Lynchburg, according to the Jack Daniel's website. The website explains that "Jack Daniel, founder of Jack Daniel's Distillery was befriended by a local lay preacher and moonshine distiller named Rev. Dan Call and began learning the distilling trade as a teenager from Call and his stillhand Nearest Green." Reverend Dan Call was the ancestor of one of Wilkes County's most famous moonshiners, Willie Clay Call of North Wilkesboro, who played a major role in the development of the state's great moonshine legacy. Brad

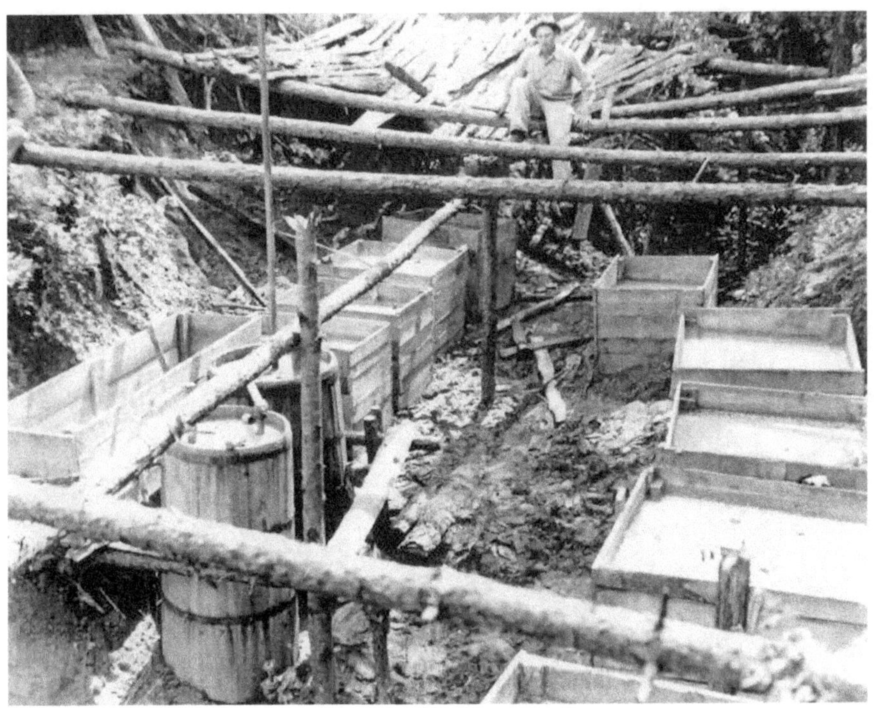

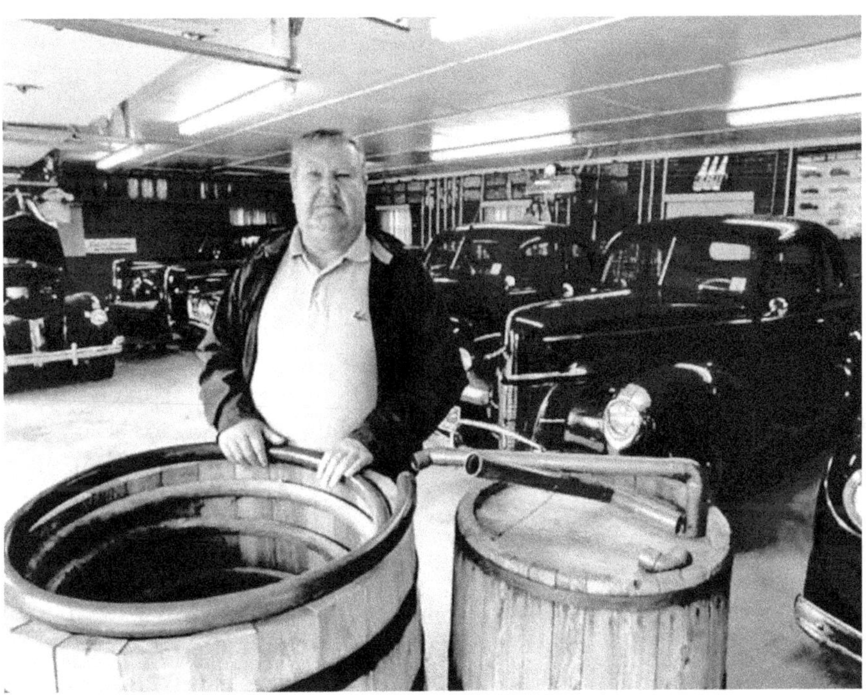

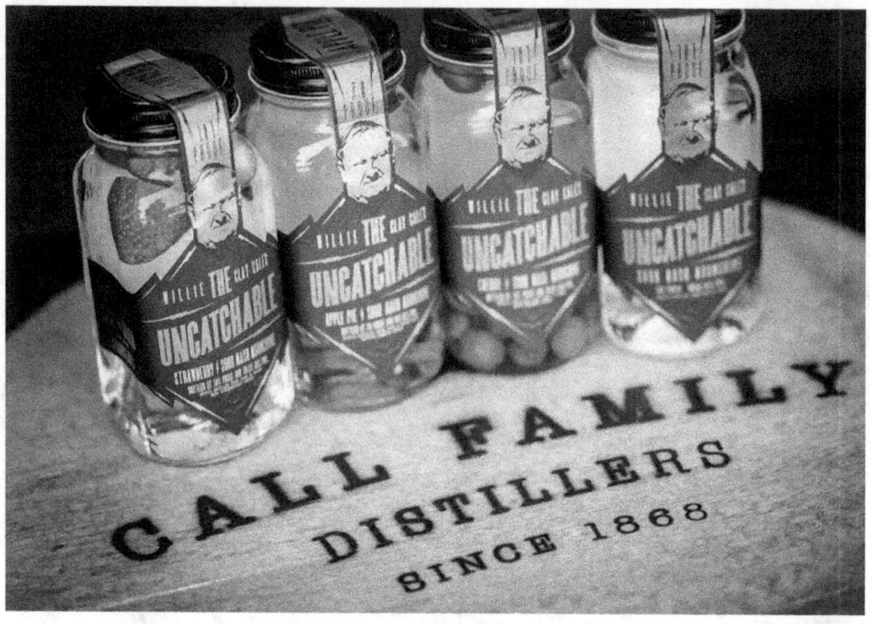

This is a display of some of the products available at the Call Family Distillery in Wilkesboro, North Carolina. *Courtesy of Brad Call, Call Family Distillers.*

Previous page, top: This large underground still was found in the Call section of Wilkes County around 1950. *Courtesy of Brad Call, Call Family Distillers.*

Previous page, bottom: Willie Clay Call was one of North Carolina's most famous moonshiners. He made and hauled high-quality moonshine out of Wilkes County for many years as a means of supporting his family. He is shown here in front of a Wilkes County whiskey still with his fleet of 1940 Fords in the background. *Courtesy of Brad Call, Call Family Distillers.*

Call, a nephew of Willie Clay Call, stated that his uncle "learned the craft of distilling from his father, Willie Simon Call, who had learned it from his father." Brian Call, son of Willie Clay Call, explained, "My father's favorite whiskey car was a 1961 Chrysler New Yorker with a five-hundred-horsepower motor. The car would hold about 130 jugs of moonshine and my father knew how to drive it." Call further explained that "a federal agent once described my father as being uncatchable when it came to driving his car."

Brad Call further explained, "My uncle was very serious when he stated that we were not bootleggers—we were moonshiners. When he retired from moonshining he would share his extensive knowledge of the history and culture of moonshine with people at local malls and gatherings. He

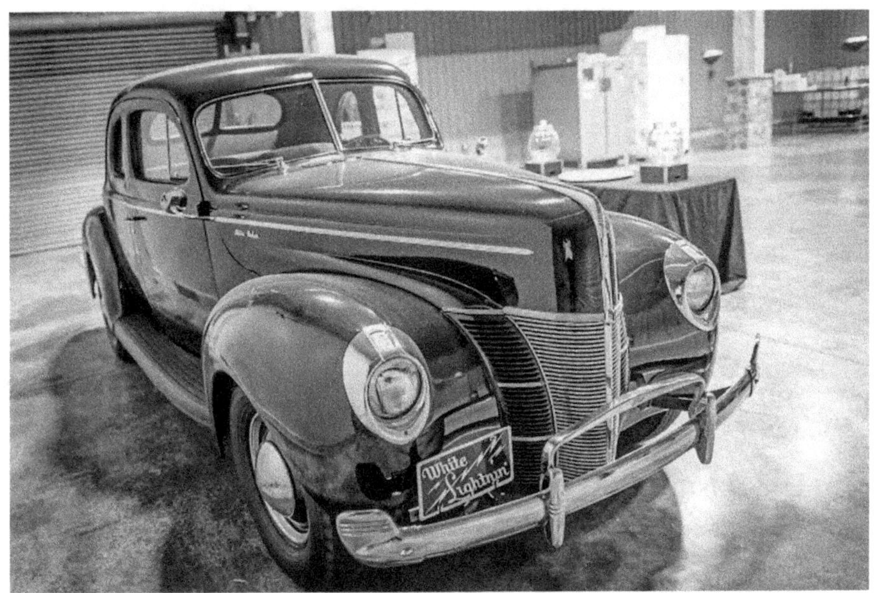

Once used to haul moonshine, this 1940 Ford is on display at Call Family Distillers in Wilkesboro, North Carolina. *Courtesy of Brad Call, Call Family Distillers.*

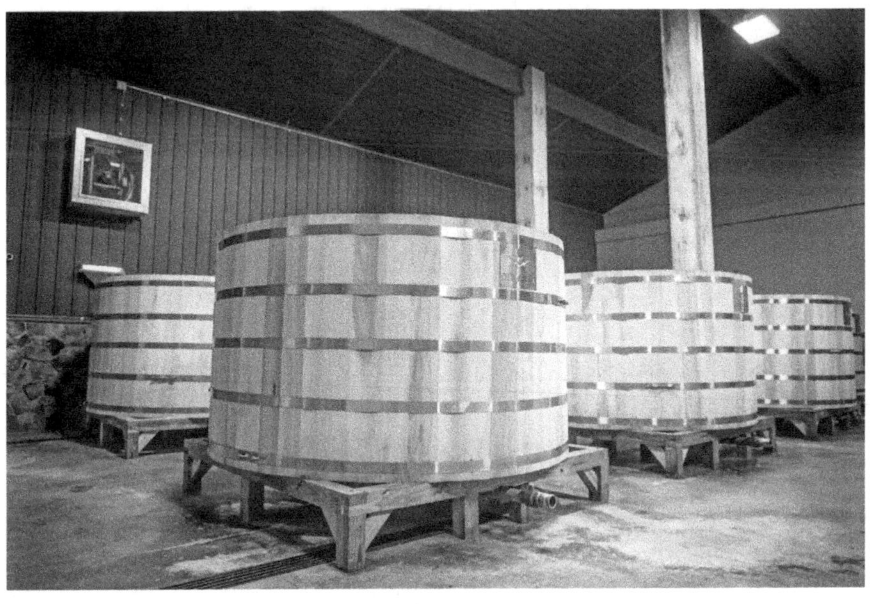

Some of the mash tanks at Call Family Distillers in Wilkesboro, North Carolina. *Courtesy of Brad Call, Call Family Distillers.*

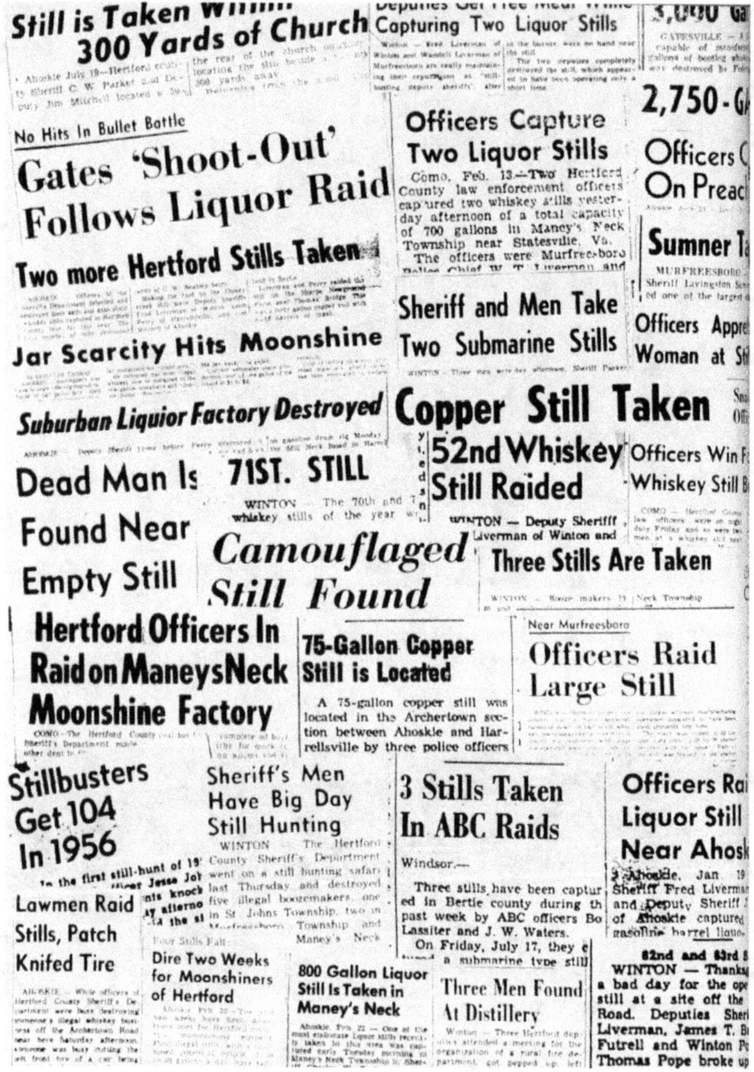

Still is Taken Within 300 Yards of Church

Capturing Two Liquor Stills

2,750-Ga

No Hits In Bullet Battle

Gates 'Shoot-Out' Follows Liquor Raid

Officers Capture Two Liquor Stills

Como, Feb. 13—Two Hertford County law enforcement officers captured two whiskey stills yesterday afternoon of a total capacity of 700 gallons in Maney's Neck Township near Statesville, Va. The officers were Murfreesboro

Officers On Preac

Two more Hertford Stills Taken

Sumner Ta

Sheriff and Men Take Two Submarine Stills

Officers Appre Woman at St

Jar Scarcity Hits Moonshine

Suburban Liquior Factory Destroyed

Copper Still Taken

Dead Man Is Found Near Empty Still

71ST. STILL

WINTON — The 70th and 71st whiskey stills of the year

52nd Whiskey Still Raided

WINTON — Deputy Sheriff Liverman of Winton and

Officers Win F Whiskey Still B

Camouflaged Still Found

Three Stills Are Taken

Hertford Officers In Raid on Maneys Neck Moonshine Factory

75-Gallon Copper Still is Located

A 75-gallon copper still was located in the Archertown section between Ahoskie and Harrellsville by three police officers

Near Murfreesboro

Officers Raid Large Still

Stillbusters Get 104 In 1956

Sheriff's Men Have Big Day Still Hunting

WINTON — The Hertford County Sheriff's Department went on a still hunting safari last Thursday and destroyed five illegal boozemakers, one in St. Johns Township, two in Murfreesboro Township and Maney's Neck

3 Stills Taken In ABC Raids

Windsor.—

Three stills have been captured in Bertie county during the past week by ABC officers Bo Lassiter and J. W. Waters. On Friday, July 17, they found a submarine type still

Officers Raid Liquor Still Near Ahoskie

Ahoskie, Jan. 19 — Sheriff Fred Liverman and Deputy Sheriff of Ahoskie captured

Lawmen Raid Stills, Patch Knifed Tire

Dire Two Weeks for Moonshiners of Hertford

800 Gallon Liquor Still Is Taken in Maney's Neck

Three Men Found At Distillery

62nd and 63rd

WINTON — Thanks a bad day for the operator of a still at a site off the Road. Deputies Sheriff Liverman, James T. B Futrell and Winton P Thomas Pope broke up

Newspaper headlines about moonshine. *Courtesy of Frank Stephenson Jr.*

also helped the town promote its heritage and tourism." Willie Clay Call, who was a friend and contemporary of Junior Johnson and one of North Carolina's most famous moonshiners, died in August 2012 and was interred in the Oak Forest Baptist Church Cemetery in Wilkesboro, North Carolina.

BIBLIOGRAPHY

Adams, Kevin. *North Carolina Waterfalls: A Hiking and Photography Guide.* Winston-Salem, NC: John F. Blair Publisher, 2005.

Bass, Misty, Christy Earp and Jennifer Peta. *Wilkes County, North Carolina.* Charleston, SC: Arcadia Publishing, 2007.

Behr, Edward. *Prohibition: Thirteen Years That Changed America.* New York: Arcade Publishing, 2011.

Berry, Marjorie Ann. *Legendary Locals of Elizabeth City.* Charleston, SC: Arcadia Publishing, 2014.

Bondurant, Matt. *The Wettest County in the World.* New York: Simon and Schuster, 2008.

Bowling, Lewis. *Granville County North Carolina.* Charleston, SC: The History Press, 2007.

Carter, Joseph E. *Damn the Alligators.* Albemarle, NC: Joseph E. Carter, 1989.

———. *Shortcuts to Justice.* Albemarle, NC: SSI Publications, 1999.

Cook, Allen. *Moonshine, Murder & Mountaineers: The Wildest County in America.* Middletown, DE: Chestnut Ridge Publishing, 2014.

Cooper, Horton. *North Carolina Mountain Folklore and Miscellany.* Murfreesboro, NC: Johnson Publishing, 1972.

Dabney, Joseph Earl. *More Mountain Spirits.* Asheville, NC: Bright Mountain Books, 1980.

———. *Mountain Spirits.* New York: Charles Scribner's Sons, 1974.

Davis, Hubert. *The Great Dismal Swamp.* Murfreesboro, NC: Johnson Publishing, 1971.

———. *Myths and Legends of the Great Dismal Swamp*. Murfreesboro, NC: Johnson Publishing, 1981.

Flood, Dudley E., and Ben Watford. *You Can't Fall Off the Floor*. Bloomington, IN: Author House, 2009.

Hairr, John. *Images of Harnett County, North Carolina*. Charleston, SC: Arcadia Publishing, 1999.

Haskell, David, and Colin Spoelman. *The Kings County Distillery Guide to Urban Moonshining: How to Make and Drink Whiskey*. New York: Abrams Books, 2013.

Higgins, Tom, and Stebe Wald. *Junior Johnson: Brave in Life*. Glastonbury, CT: David Bull Publishing, 1999.

Jester, Tom Wilson. *Popcorn Sutton: The Making and Marketing of a Hillbilly Hero*. Knoxville, TN: Dudenbostel Photography, 2011

Johnson, F. Roy. *The Roanoke-Chowan Story*. Murfreesboro, NC: Johnson Publishing, 1965.

———. *Tales from Old Carolina*. Murfreesboro, NC: Johnson Publishing, 1966.

Johnson, Randy. *Hiking North Carolina*. Guilford, CT: Rowman and Littlefield, 2007.

Jolly, Harley E. *Blue Ridge Parkway*. Knoxville: University of Tennessee Press, 1969.

———. *That Magnificent Army of Youth and Peace: The Civilian Conservation Corps in North Carolina, 1933–1942*. North Carolina Department of Archives and History, Raleigh, 2007.

Joyce, Jaime. *Moonshine: A Cultural History of America's Infamous Liquor*. Minnesota, MN: Zenith Press, 2014.

Miller, Wilbur R. *Revenuers and Moonshiners*. Chapel Hill: University of North Carolina Press, 1991.

Peck, Garrett. *Prohibition in Washington, D.C.* Charleston, SC: The History Press, 2011.

Pierce, Daniel. *Real NASCAR: White Lightning, Red Clay and Big Bill France*. Chapel Hill: University of North Carolina Press, 2010.

Pierce, Dan. *Corn from a Jar: Moonshining and the Great Smokey Mountains*. Gatlinburg, TN: Great Smokey Mountain Association, 2013.

Pitzer, Sara. *Off the Beaten Path: North Carolina*. Guilford, CT: Morris Book Publishing, 2012.

Pogue, Dennis J. *Founding Spirits: George Washington and the Beginnings of the American Whiskey Industry*. Buena Vista, VA: Harbor Books, 2011.

Powell, Jack Allen. *A Dying Art*. Catskill, NY: Press-Tige Publishing, 1996.

Simpson, Bland. *The Great Dismal: A Carolinian's Swamp Memoir*. Chapel Hill: University of North Carolina Press, 1998.

Spivak, Mark. *Moonshine Nation: The Art of Creating Cornbread in a Bottle.* Guilford, CT: Lyons Press, 2014.

Stephenson, Frank. *Carolina Moonshine Raiders*. Murfreesboro, NC: Meherrin River Press, 2001.

———. *Chowan Beach: Remembering an African American Resort.* Charleston, SC: The History Press, 2006.

———. *Chowan College*. Charleston, SC: Arcadia Publishing, 2004.

———. *Herring Fisherman*. Charleston, SC: The History Press, 2007.

———. *Images of Hertford County, North Carolina*. Charleston, SC: Arcadia Publishing, 2003.

———. *The Murfreesboro Railroad Company*. Murfreesboro, NC: Meherrin River Press, 1996.

———. *Parker's Ferry, Hertford County, North Carolina*. Murfreesboro, NC: Meherrin River Press, 1995.

———. *Tunis, North Carolina*. Murfreesboro, NC: Meherrin River Press, 2009.

Stewart, Bruce. *King of the Moonshiners: Lewis R. Redmond in Fact and Fiction*. Knoxville: University of Tennessee Press, 2009.

Stick, David. *Dare County: A History*. Raleigh: North Carolina Department of Archives and History, 1970.

Sullivan, Perry. *Lost Flowers: True Stories of the Moonshine King, Percy Flowers*. Chicago: Createspace, 2013.

Sutton, Sky. *Daddy Moonshine: The Story of Marvin Popcorn Sutton*. Northampton, MA: Sky Sutton, 2008

Tate, Suzanne. *Logs & Moonshine: Tales of Buffalo City, North Carolina*. Nags Head, NC: Nags Head Art, 2000.

Taylor, Rosser Howard. *Carolina Crossroads*. Murfreesboro, NC: Johnson Publishing, 1966.

Thompson, Neal. *Driving with the Devil: Southern Moonshine, Detroit Wheels and the Birth of NASCAR*. New York: Three Rivers Press, 2006.

Traylor, Waverly. *The Great Dismal Swamp in Myth and Legend*. Pittsburgh, PA: Rose Dog Books, 2010.

Turner, Johnny. *Wheels and Moonshine*. Middletown, DE: Kindle Books, 2015.

Wilkinson, Alec. *Moonshine: A Life in Pursuit of White Liquor*. New York: Alfred A. Knopf, 1985.

INDEX

INDEX

ABOUT THE AUTHORS

Barbara Nichols Mulder and Frank Stephenson Jr. are longtime employees of Chowan University in Murfreesboro, North Carolina. Both grew up in rural Hertford County, North Carolina, when moonshine was big business and moonshine stills could be found anywhere. While growing up, they heard numerous moonshine stories and knew people who were involved in moonshine one way or another. Their personal experience of and deep appreciation for the rural southern life experience was the catalyst for their writing this book. They have collaborated on numerous other books on rural life in North Carolina, including *Eastern North Carolina Farming*, which was published by Arcadia Publishing in November 2014.

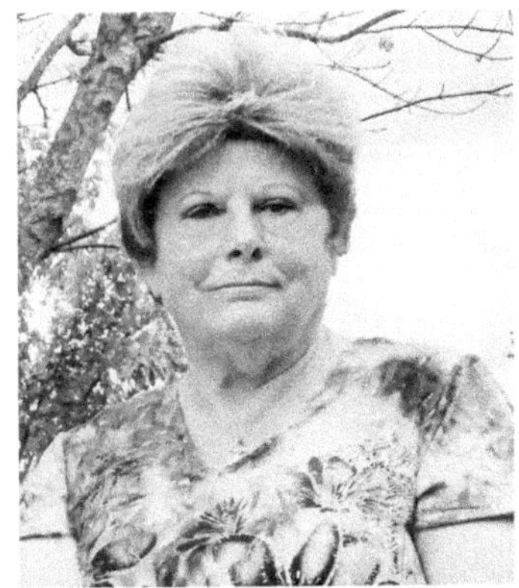

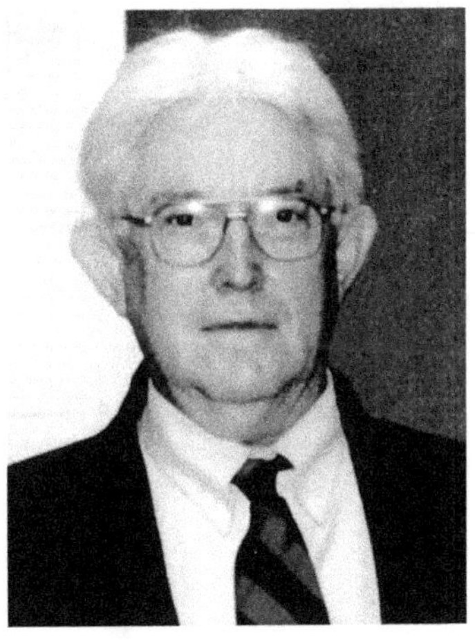

Visit us at
www.historypress.net

This title is also available as an e-book

www.ingramcontent.com/pod-product-compliance
Lightning Source LLC
LaVergne TN
LVHW010949100826
845153LV00002B/172

* 9 7 8 1 5 4 0 2 1 4 1 0 2 *